Meditation is Magnificent Medication

Meditation is Magnificent Medication

Malak Morgan

WisdomSpring Publishing
P.O. Box 621101
Oviedo, FL 32762-1101
United States of America
Book editions produced by Kindle Direct Publishing for WisdomSpring Publishing. kdp.amazon.com

Library of Congress Control Number: 2022909761
ISBN: 978-0-9829483-0-9
First Edition: 2023

To my Dad
who is in heaven, who taught me the principles of Christianity, and who taught me the love of reading, and that it is knowledge that brings light to the mind.

To my Mom
who taught me to pray the Psalms, and who is still supporting me and my family by her fervent prayers and supplications.

To my Father-in-Law
who showed me another level of faith, accuracy, and persistence; who supports me and my family with his fervent prayers.

To my Mother-in-Law
who frees my time for writing, and who is great help for us and our boys. All the thanksgiving words are not enough to tell of her help and support.

To my Wife
who is my helpmate in the journey of life.
I asked the Lord for help and He sent my wife.

To my Boys
who are the best gift from God and who are the reason I write, so that they can have God's given knowledge.

Table of Contents

Preface

Every school, college and university starts with an orientation with the intent that students and scholars know what to expect and how to succeed. We are in great need to read the orientation manual for this world, so we can take heed of our life on earth and journey successfully to our home in heaven. The Bible is the orientation manual for our life. We are on an earthly journey, and one day every one of us will give an account of what he did while on this journey. Our actions and reactions that are guided by the Holy Spirit and filled with love will determine our reward in Heaven. God has provided us with spiritual laws and Divine commandments throughout the Bible. The grace of God always provides for man to apply these laws and commandments with the end result being a life lived reflecting Christ - virtuous on earth, and with Him in heaven at the end of this journey.

Questions Need Answers

Why do some attend church and hear powerful sermons about love, yet still live in hatred with their relatives? Why do some have all luxuries in life, and still cannot extend the hand of giving or charity to those in need? Why do some have a high paying job with a great title, and still feel insecure? Why do some have all the facilities of life, but still are not happy? Why do good holiday seasons come and some families cannot gather together in peace to spend beautiful celebrations like Christmas and Thanksgiving? Why do children repeat the same mistakes as their parents? Why did the parents not warn their children not to make the same mistakes? Why is there division between the parents and their children? Why is there anxiety and depression and suicide in the world? Why is there divorce between couples that lived in love together for many years and have precious memories and grown children? Why is there division between the spouses and their parents-in-law? Why do some need more time and energy, but still waste what they have? Why do some want to be healthy, but still eat junk food? Why do some know what they are doing is wrong, but still are doing it? Why are some students smart in playing games, but their grades don't reflect their high mental capabilities?

Answers and Clues

The answers for all these questions can be summarized in two parts. First: the human adversary is behind all these divisions and deviations of human behavior. Second: the words of God did not go deep enough into our minds to be in effect. There is no one who followed and applied God's spiritual laws and commandments who did not succeed in life. However, the challenge arises from how to put these commandments into effect. To put God's laws and commandments into consistent action, they must be ingrained in our subconscious minds. Our conscious mind is the receptor for instructions, and subconscious mind the sender of actions. Most of us think that just the mere listening to sermons in a church will put God's laws into actions. This is absolutely not so! While this is the thought of many, others think that merely reading God's instructions will put them into effect. It will not! God's words are like seeds that need to be planted in good ground. The good ground is the subconscious mind, which will retain God's words, allow it to grow and put it into actions. Only then will God's words bear fruit. Among the fruit will be success in our marriages, raising children, careers, healing, charity, harmony, and glorifying God.

Meditation on God's word is the planting of these seeds into our subconscious minds. This book is based on the process of cultivating God's words in our minds. It is based on vivid, personal experience that combines spiritual principles, testimony, analysis and observation of human behaviors. This combination is placed in a simple, concise, but still rich text to comprehend and apply in our day to day routines.

The goal of meditation on the words of God is to become Christ-like persons. This becoming is a pilgrimage based on taking carefully selected biblical verses that characterize a Christ-like person. Then these verses are phrased simply, concisely, in present tense, and personalized, which in turn form affirmations. The meditator recites these affirmations, which means saying them to himself again and again until the grace of God establishes them in his heart, changing and developing him into a Christ-like person. The meditation presented in this manuscript is different and absolutely separate from any kind of meditation that invites any supernatural power. The name of the meditation shared in this book is *In Christ Meditation*.

What Is Unique about This Book?

Many readers think they will return to a book and try to apply the knowledge they gained from it. However, most of the time that doesn't happen. Most of us move on and read another book. What is unique about this book is that it gives you only one page, a template, that lives with you as long as you want. That page can make the change of your life. At this point, it is highly recommended to check the back of this book. The template of *In Christ Meditation* is presented there. Kindly detach it from the book or print it if you received the electronic version of the book, make copies and put them into plastic sheets. Keep these copies handy and start to use these affirmations. It is highly recommended to recite audibly the affirmations. As you take the journey of reading the book and reciting these affirmations, the grace of God will change you into a Christ-like person, living a virtuous, successful, well-balanced, fulfilling life.

The book is the product of intensive work done during the 2020 pandemic. The real evidence of the need to read the book is that, while there is a global challenge because of the pandemic and its vast effect worldwide, applying the principles of the book helped me to rise above this challenge and put this manuscript together. Now the fruit is between your hands - *Meditation is Magnificent Medication*. May the grace of God help the readers to understand the spiritual principles contained in the book and get the benefits of them.

The Author

1: Principles of Life

(1) There is only One Spiritual Sovereignty in the whole world, that is God. God is Omnipresent, Omniscient, and Omnipotent. He inspires every man to do good, to have true peace, to have harmony, and to have success. Then what about the Adversary? He is the fallen angel that by his own will became the opponent to God. The Adversary plays a major role in all hatred, anxiety and despair in the world. How is God Omnipresent yet these concerns exist in man's life? The Adversary can exist in man's life when man willingly excludes God's lordship from his life, or unknowingly forgets the existence of God. Every man must determine for himself who he will follow in his life.

The first and foremost of a man's wisdom is the fear of God, from which comes the ability to discern God's voice from the Adversary's. We are in great need to have our ears attentive to God's voice and differentiate it from the Adversary's voice. We need to listen to that calm, soft voice in our hearts. It is the voice of God. But never follow that harsh, loud voice; it is the voice of the Adversary. By God's grace, the more we read God's words, the more we are able to recognize His voice, and the more we can discern the Adversary's voice. The Bible says, "Those who by reason of use have their senses exercised to discern both good and evil" (Hebrews 5:14). The Adversary gives us false security. He tempts us to depend on our material possessions. Sometimes he says, "Nobody is as good as you." Sometimes he says, "What will happen? Just do it." Other times, he brings into our minds despair of any change to improve ourselves, or doubt of God's love and care for us. Often the Adversary rushes us to do things without pondering the consequences. When we hear the Adversary's voice and recognize any of these kinds of influences, we need to ponder our actions and reactions.

We need to remember that our lives are precious. When we have Christ in our conscious mind, we can discern and examine every thought that comes to our mind. Is this thought from God or the Adversary? A great deal of wisdom lies in one's self-examining his thoughts. We need to ask the Lord to have mercy on us and help us to avoid the Adversary's traps. To help ourselves in this regard, it is wisdom to repeat very often, "Lord, have mercy upon me and help me." This principle of wisdom is a very important and fundamental one. We will keep referring to it as we go in this manuscript.

(2) Life has three fundamental principles:

a. Life is a gift from God to proceed and succeed in fulfilling His plan for our lives.
b. Life is the sum of our choices.
c. Life is the reflection of man's thoughts. If we equip our minds with good thoughts, we will make good choices, which in turn will reflect in a good life.

It is astonishing that in these days many of us don't know these principles. No wonder the majority waste their lives in trivial things not related to the purpose of their lives.

While life has these principles, it also has two vital pillars: time and energy. Time is the only factor in life that no one can store nor retrieve. Ponder how you handle your time and you will know the quality of your life. As an example, a most common saying but ever ignored is that "time is money." So if we waste our time, we are wasting money. It is wisdom to use time to build knowledge and skills; hence, this can greatly benefit one's finances.

Energy is the factor that the whole world seeks after. Everyone needs and wishes for more. The widespread paradox is that people tend to waste the energy they have.

We waste our energy and time in social media, gossip, negative emotions, television, and other things that deplete energy and time. Before we ask for more energy, we need to ask ourselves what we do with the energy we have. Even if we get more energy but do not know how to manage what we have, we will end up with no beneficial change. When we have wisdom, we will know how to allocate our time and our energy, and then our lives will become magnificent.

(3) We humans are like branches in one big tree called humanity. There is one God, there is one human race, and there is one enemy. Meditation helps us see, value, and respond in Christ-like ways to these bonds among our brothers and sisters in humanity. Once man recognizes this simple fact, there will be a shift in his way of thinking and in his daily interactions. One thing we all want in common is a good life. A man's good life is the fruit of wisdom and applying God's principles. Meditation on God's principles makes a man wise and able to have a good life.

(4) Transgression against God's commandments causes man to fear. It is a terrible thing to live in fear. Before we sin, every one of us needs to ask himself this simple and deep question: Am I able to live in fear? When we sin, it means that we follow the Adversary. Sin brings the worst fear. Fear is the result of doing something against God's commandments that hurts our relationship with Him. The root of fear was clearly exhibited in the book of Genesis, "After Adam and Eve ate from the fruit of the tree then the eyes of both of them were opened, and they knew that they were naked. When God called Adam, Adam said, 'I heard Your voice in the garden, and I was afraid because I was naked; and I hid myself'" (Genesis 3:10). In these days, we sin and as a result we fear, then look for medications to suppress the fear. We tend next to go to a physician trying to find remedy for this fear, which ends by our living on anxiety meds. We become legalized addicts.

The true remedy is that we need to confess and admit our sin, and God will forgive us. "If we confess our sins, He is faithful and just to forgive us our sins and to cleanse us from all unrighteousness" (1 John 1:9). The amazing thing is that we look at people who lived in the past and see them as fear-free, saying their days were better than ours. The fact is that we have an incredibly better life, but we do not want to get rid of our sins and our fears.

(5) The beginning of our advancement process is to know who we are. The following facts sum up what a man is. A man is a son of God after choosing to believe in the Lord Jesus Christ (John 1:12). A man is a spiritual being having a physical journey on earth, starting at physical birth and continuing in eternity. A man is the quality of his thoughts. Knowing oneself is the starting point in everyone's life to steer himself to what is better. A man is different from others in that he sees and experiences things from his own mental attitude and optimism or pessimism. Man's mental attitude towards circumstances, not the circumstances themselves, makes him happy or miserable. Man's positive attitude toward circumstances can steer him toward positive outcomes. How we react to circumstances reveals who we are. Choosing positive mental attitudes can change the outcomes of these circumstances. Defeat is not a defeat unless we accept it as reality. Every one of us has the power, through the grace of God, to change his reality. We can live in true nobility by continuous and endless self-improvement and by being transformed from what we were before. Only those who recognize that Christ lives within and only those who believe that Christ can conform them to His image, can change their defeat to ever brighter success.

(6) True poverty is not the lack of money. It is the inability to recognize the truth. The truth is that only through Christ can a man overcome the Adversary and have a good life. The truth is that Christ came to earth to save us and not to judge us. "For God

did not send His Son into the world to condemn the world, but that the world through Him might be saved" (John 3:17). By Christ coming to earth and living in us, we are empowered to become a decisive and dynamic force in our success. We need to ask to receive, we must seek to find, we must knock and it will be opened for us. Our thoughts steer our actions to success or failure. Failure and poverty are not determined by circumstances. The origin of these are laid down deep in the thoughts. True poverty is the inability to recognize truth. True poverty has nothing to do with not having a big bank account, a luxurious house or expensive car. A man could have all luxuries of life and still be poor. To be a true winner in life, to enjoy true wealth, we need to know and live as a Christ-like noble person, never lose hope, and never quit. Meditation on Christ is an absolute gift from God. It's the ever great tool that can transform a man to Christ-like character. Through meditation a man can truly know Christ and this is the greatest wealth a man can have.

(7) Suffering and pain are natural aspects of life. They are the pressure of the Potter's hand on the clay to make magnificent art crafts. For most, hardships are the shortest way to mindful life. Those who encounter suffering tend to ponder the value of life. We all want to live a life that is suffering-free and pleasure-granted. Yet if Christ came to earth and suffered, why would we not suffer? Pleasures are transient and often followed by pain. True and lasting pleasure is in self-control and overcoming passions and worldly desires. Hence the mind is clear, pure, and focused on Christ-like spiritual matters and meditation.

The paradox of life is either win-win or lose-lose, with no happy medium. Those who spend their lives in pleasure that is vain and perishable, lose their lives here and for eternity. Didn't Solomon the Wise say this a long time ago, "I have seen all the works that are done under the sun; and indeed, all is vanity and grasping for the wind" (Ecclesiastes 1:12)? Those who spend their lives in self-control and virtue that is lasting, win their lives here and for eternity.

(8) God created man in His image and everything He has created was good (Genesis 1:27,31). Every man was created to be a good man; however, man yielded his free will to the Adversary. When we encounter a man who behaves badly, we need to remember that he has given himself into the hand of the Adversary. We need to remember what Christ taught us to do, "But I say to you, love your enemies, bless those who curse you, do good to those who hate you, and pray for those who spitefully use you and persecute you" (Matthew 5:44). Silence, smile, apology, soft answers make a man avoid problems and can resolve many conflicts with those used by the Adversary to hurt us. The irony is that most of us do what is opposite to what Christ taught us. We still focus on the person himself and forget the hidden and unseen negative power that drove that man to bad behaviors. In addition, we ought to pray for such people. We need to pray for them because Christ taught us to do so. We need to pray that we ourselves are saved from the evil deeds. We need to pray that they may come to self-realization, come to Christ, leave their evil deeds, and value humanity.

(9) There are many ways we use the word "love", and many kinds of love. Love is the answer of every problem. If you love God, you will follow His commandments. If you love a class, you will study hard and get good grades. If you love your job, you will excel in it and get promoted. If you love your spouse, you will strive to make him or her happy. If you love your son, you will discipline him and raise him in the fear and the love of the Lord. If you love yourself, you will seek wisdom. If you love to attain Christ-like character, you will put faith in Him, meditate on His words and obey Him until the grace of God makes you to reach Christ-like spiritual

personality. Only then will you see your life and the whole world from His noble prospective.

(10) Through the virtue of humbleness, a man escapes the traps of the devil. Humility is power, not humiliation. *It was pride that changed angels into devils; it is humility that makes men as angels.*[1] The Adversary has succeeded in convincing us that humility is weakness. As a result, most of us are driven by pride and arrogance. We forget that pride destroyed angels and arrogance destroyed great historical figures. We have division and hardships in our careers, marriage, business, and friendships, because we lost our humbleness. The truth is that with humbleness there are blessings. Wisdom, honor, and happiness are the results of humbleness. Humility is power and strength against the traps of the devil. Humbleness starts in the thoughts and is expressed in our behavior and our deeds. To motivate ourselves to humility, we need to remember these two verses, "Pride goes before destruction, and a haughty spirit before a fall" (Proverbs 16:18), and "The fear of the Lord is the instruction of wisdom, and before honor is humility" (Proverbs 15:33).

(11) The free will is a precious gift from God. If you do the opposite to what you want to do, kindly assess who has your will. It is not Christ who wants you to do what is against your will when your will is to please God. It is the devil. You need to determine to free your will to live as a Christ-like person. Only those who do what they actually want to do have a good grip of their will. Only those who eat healthy food have free will. Only those who buy what they need have a firm grasp of their will. If you do what you do not want to do, you do not have a free will. The only way to keep your free will is give it to God who granted it to you. He can keep it safe from the hands of the Adversary. When you recognize this, you can say, "Your will be done" (Matthew 6:10). A great wisdom of one's gaining his lost free will is to expose his thoughts

to God. God knows our thoughts; however, one thing He will never do is violate our free will. "I call heaven and earth as witnesses today against you, that I have set before you life and death, blessing and cursing; therefore choose life, that both you and your descendants may live" (Deuteronomy 30:19). He gave us this right and will never violate it. So, with your free will, take any disturbing thoughts and ask His help about them, but never let them take root within. For instance, if we keep an apple closed in a plastic bag and not exposed to air, it will decay. Despite that, we may think that the apple is still clean from the outside. Thoughts are alike. They can rot our minds because some of them are deceiving. Now if you do not have peace about a thought, do not pursue it. It is better to wait and test that thought than to pursue it and regret it for a long time or maybe for the rest of your life. We always need to remember this wisdom, "There is a way that seems right to a man, but its end is the way of death" (Proverbs 14:12).

(12) Inner peace is a way God has to tell every one of us His will. If you don't have this peace don't proceed. If you don't have God's peace, do not marry that person. If you do not have His inner peace, don't buy that house. One aspect of absolute wisdom is to do what God wants us to do in our lives. He will equip us and help us to do so. The challenge that every one of us meets when making a decision is, how do I know what God wants me to do? For example, Which career should I pursue? Which house should I buy? Who is the right spouse from God? Sometimes God sends us messages and we misunderstand them.

A man applied for another job as he was not happy in his current job. As this man was trying to find God's will, he asked for prayer from his family to reach a decision. God sent him many messages that He should not leave his current job. He stated that not all his family was agreeing on this new position. He did not have inner peace about it. However, he accepted the new position under the concept of taking a risk and "the grass is greener on the other side." Of course, there were some advantages in the new position. After he started the new position, he found that these advantages were not as he expected and the new job was more stressful than the previous one. It was too late to go back to his old job. He finally understood and interpreted God's messages to him.

In analyzing what happened, there are two important things needed to find out to know what God wants us to do: 1) Inner peace to proceed. Always be sure to have true godly peace before pursuing anything. If we do not have this inner peace, it is prudent not to proceed with anything. Godly peace is the green light to move forward in any matter of our lives. If you do not have this peace, do not waste your time and energy trying things you don't have the Divine help to do. To have this peace, always make this request in your prayer: "According to Your will, O Lord, fill my heart with Your peace." This will keep us safe from false peace and unbearable consequences. 2) Family consensus is an important sign to proceed. It is seriously imprudent to do something that your family is not happy about. Family consensus is another way God sends us messages of His will. To be in a state of happiness and peace is to do what God wants for your goodness and success.

(13) You can change your world by changing your words. You can change words by changing your thoughts. You can change your thoughts by letting Christ be in your mind.

An early thirties man was entrapped for some time by the thought that he was getting old and would not find the right spouse. Through prayers, God guided him into a deeper understanding of these two important verses: "According to your faith let it be to you" (Matthew 9:29). The second verse: "Ask, and it will be given to you; seek, and you will find; knock, and it will be opened to you" (Matthew 7:7). So he wrote on a piece of paper what characteristics he was looking for in his spouse-to-be. He kept this paper in his Bible and continued praying for that spouse to show up. He made an agreement with himself that every time he was about to say, "I am not finding the right spouse," to stop, and say, "God is sending to me the right spouse." Two years went by as he held his faith, and the Lord sent him the right spouse. When this man started to proclaim faith and changed his words, he changed his world.

(14) The perfection of wisdom is to live each day as if it is the last day before we step into eternity. This wisdom will make us live in continual repentance and pursue the life of virtue. Those who preceded us to eternity did not know their last days.

There are types of death. The physical death is the release of the spirit from the body and transitioning to eternity. The spiritual death is the living in sin. A man who lives in sin is dead spiritually. If this man dies physically, he will spend his eternity in separation from God. Most of us forget the fact that spiritual death leads to eternal death. This forgetting comes from the busy lifestyle and the cares of this world. It can also come from intentional disregard for God. Since it is a devastating matter for any man to spend his eternity separated from God, it is important to live in continual repentance.

A godly Sunday school teacher at the beginning of each new season used to visit the attendees of his class. As he was serving adolescent students, he faced many challenges. One of these challenges was that one particular student used to speak with harsh words when the teacher called or went to visit him. This adolescent was completely influenced by the Adversary to go astray from God and not to repent. Despite the fact that part of the Sunday school ministry is for the teachers to visit their students, this teacher decided not to visit this adolescent, wanting to avoid his harsh words and spiteful dealings. One day, the teacher met with his own spiritual mentor, who asked him about the visitation aspect of his service. The mentor inquired about not only visitation in general, but also in particular about that adolescent, who had stopped coming to the church and Sunday school. The teacher told his mentor that he had stopped visiting this youth, explaining the unpleasant behaviors he'd experienced. The mentor said to the teacher, "Are you giving up your stewardship? If this youth dies in his sins, he will be in eternal hell" The teacher decided to visit the youth again. It happened that when the teacher visited, the young man opened the door and welcomed him cheerfully. The teacher asked the youth about the reason for the change. "For the last few days, I felt sick and scared of death. I started to ponder where I would go if I die. I wanted to repent, but my sins were an obstacle for going back to God. I kept asking God to show me that He loves me, and here you are just knocking my door!" The Sunday School teacher deeply pondered what could have happened if he had not come this time to the young man. He would have been left as a prey to the Adversary, believing the lie that God did not love him. If he had died, he would've been in eternal separation from God. As the Holy Spirit lives in us, He will equip us and empower us to live in continual repentance. It is absolute wisdom to make sure of our eternity at every single moment of our lives.

(15) When we act from a heart full of wisdom, we will avoid mistakes. To fill our hearts with wisdom, we need to fill our hearts with God. To fill our hearts with God, we need to meditate on God's words. Despite this truth, the majority of us act from fear. Fear is a negative feeling that can come upon any of us who perceive unpleasant consequences. There is a natural fear that God created in us so we avoid danger. An example of this is the fear that if I walk barefoot on hot sand, my feet will get burned. And there is a fear which is a trap of the devil. This type of fear can be emotional dark clouds that can lead to not perceiving actual reality. That fear

can paralyze brain functions including right reasoning, critical thinking, sound judgment, calm concentration, and genuine enthusiasm. It blocks beautiful emotions such as love, ambition, and hope. It annuls thought control and directing one's energy to success and prosperity. As a result of fear, we tend to change our behavior, actions, and reactions.

A college student was entrapped in the second type of fear. He was enrolled to major in engineering. After a few semesters, he changed his major to business. He kept changing his major until he had accumulated a lot of classes but none that could qualify him for any certain degree. Not only this, he also reached the student loans limit he could receive. One day at his college, there was a workshop at which an entrepreneur had been invited to speak about his success. The entrepreneur encouraged the students to study what they liked and never fear to take risks. As the student followed the success tools provided by this successful man, he changed his fear. He persevered and kept facing his challenges. A few years later, I met this fellow after he finished his education and was holding a good job in one the local universities.

Submit your fears to God and receive faith instead that will direct your life to success. We always need to remember the type of spirit that we received from God, "For God has not given us a spirit of fear, but of power and of love and of a sound mind" (2 Timothy 1:7).

(16) Christ-like character is to treat people with greater love than their hatred. Meditation on God's word is one of the important practices that inspires a man to be Christ-like in character. There are many goals and objectives of meditation. One meditation can be to relieve stress and anxiety. Another meditation is to overcome illness. Despite the fact that these various types of medita-

tion are good, we indeed need a comprehensive meditation composed of all these positive aspects. The meditation presented in this manuscript is *In Christ Meditation*. It is the meditation on Christ as role model; the meditation that will equip us to live virtuous lives on earth as Christ did. This meditation is magnificent medication to the challenges, difficulties, and hardships that a man encounters in his life.

This meditation is a long, increasingly wonderful journey that starts by knowing yourself. Knowing self is learning where we are standing relative to Christ's teaching and the manner of life He wants us to live. There are many areas in which everyone needs improvement. Some are spiritual matters such as inner strength, having peace with relatives and co-workers, being successful, having a well-balanced life, positive interactions, and listening skills.

Nothing is greater than to take charge of your life. Nothing is better than becoming the master of yourself. You will be the master of yourself when Christ is the master of your mind. Always remember that self-mastery is the fruit of persistent collaborative efforts of self-discipline and self-improvement. The challenge is to realize the starting point for all these positive changes. The answer for this challenge lies in meditating on the word of God. When we meditate on the word of God, we focus our mind on His amazing character and deeds, and we experience His spectacular actions in our lives. The word of God proclaims the power of God. As every one of us needs the power of God, we are in need of continual meditation on God's power. The more we mediate on the power of God, the more we experience His power.

2: Meditation Overview

(1) What is Meditation?

The type of meditation presented here is a spiritual practice meant to ingrain specific biblical concepts in the subconscious mind. These concepts will take root in our mind. Hence after, the fruit will be the molding of our character to that of Christ. Meditation is the act of repeating certain positive statements actively and purposely until one acts and reacts accordingly, voluntarily and involuntarily. The origin of these statements is Christ's teachings, Psalms, and biblical verses that bring forth peace, comfort, and assurance.

Meditation is a sacred link between man's spirit and God. It is a noble method of recognizing God lives within. It is the real way to a strong spirit, focused mind, and healthy body. It is the ever-available tool for immense peace and positive attitude. It is a tool for great achievement; a sharp weapon to overcome calamities. It is the best shield to stay still in crisis. It is a sincere spiritual exercise which leads to getting rid of negative thoughts and harmful emotions. It is a way to promote faith. "The just shall live by faith" (Romans 1:17).

Meditation is saying to oneself biblical verses, which by hearing over and over will unlock the power of faith. When we keep reciting and hearing God's words, our minds will be filled with His words. The net result is that the mind will not have an empty spot for doubt. Once our faith is promoted by the practice of meditation, we can move the mountains in our lives. These mountains can be hardships and difficulties.

As meditation brings a man to an attachment with God in spiritual and mental union, it causes him to attain a high level of consciousness and newness of spiritual life. When a man knows Jesus Christ and determines to live in the likeness of His character, he does become a new man. "Therefore, if anyone is in Christ, he is a new creation; old things have passed away; behold, all things have become new" (2 Corinthians 5:17). Christ-like meditation keeps a man in the new state. It leads him to reject the old things and habits in his life. If these old habits surface again in one's life, through the continuous practice of meditation along with perseverance in applying Christ's principles, a man will continue in the newness of life through Christ.

(2) Fundamentals of Meditation

Whatever you constantly meditate upon, you not only will come to understand, but will grow more and more into its likeness, for it will become incorporated into your very being. It will become, in fact, your very self.[2] *We* become what we meditate on. What we meditate on becomes our essence. When we meditate on Christ, we become increasingly more Christ-like in character. When we attain Christ-like character, we overcome ourselves. When we overcome ourselves, we can overcome the world as Christ did. A man is not what he thinks of himself. A man is the sum of his thoughts. We are what we think of more frequently. We are the quality of our thoughts. If a man thinks carnal, that is, self-serving, self-centered thoughts, he takes himself to the lowest side of the scale of thoughts. If a man thinks of pure and gentle thoughts, he takes himself to the upper side of the scale of thoughts. By meditating on words that characterize our ultimate goals and hoped ideals, we drive these words deep into our subconscious mind. There they will take root and begin to create wonderful changes in our lives. These are the changes we always wanted to adopt, but may have not known how.

On a daily basis, things follow things. Life is in continuous movement. Happy are those who slow down to learn from the past to heed the future. Happy is the man who by God's grace processes life, rather than life processing him. Meditation brings us into slowing down in our lives. The more we slow down, the more we can attain spiritual awareness. The more we attain spiritual awareness, the more we are able to realize God's resources within ourselves. The more we realize God's resources within ourselves, the more God's power can manifest in our life. The more God's power manifests in our life, the more we observe amazing things happening in our lives. All that then remains is to praise God.

One of the most precious fundamentals of meditation is reviving our revered rapport with God. The worst illness that a man suffers is forgetting his initial Divine image and his future purpose. Consequently, he does not understand the ultimate meaning and value of his life. Hence, we see many of our brothers and sisters nowadays wanting to put an end to their lives. King David in the book of Psalms crystalized for us this Divine image, "You have crowned him with glory and honor. You have made him to have dominion over the works of Your hands; You have put all things under his feet" (Psalm 8:5-6). Dear reader, do we look like this image anymore? Sadly, very many of us are on medication to calm our anxiety. Most of us keep headsets plugged into our ears even when we're walking in nature. All these are pushed into our lives by the power of the Adversary and masked by different names such lifestyle or culture. Meditation brings us into a session with ourselves; consequently, we recognize our sacred rapport with the original essence of ourselves that is God, His Divine image designed into us. When we escape from ourselves then, we escape from God, for God is in ourselves. The disciple John says, "Look to yourselves..." (2 John 1:8). He encourages us to search ourselves and see where we are standing in relation to Christ and His teaching; in relation to that image God created. Do we diligently retrieve it and live it? Meditation brings us to awareness of ourselves and the image we do have. Is it the image of Christ? Or the image with which the world stained us? Meditation brings us to discover the error in our image. Then by actively seeking spiritual knowledge of Christ, we will be restored to the original Divine image through the work of the Holy Spirit.

Another important fundamental of meditation is to live in the world but not allow the world to live in us, because once we are in Christ, we are no longer of the world (John 15:19). The practice of meditation takes us from the world. It connects us with our origin that is God, the Sole Source of inspiration, wisdom, and positivity. While this is true, the practice of meditation disconnects us from the despair and the negativity of the world. The Psalmist found this great wisdom and stated in the first sentence of the Psalms, "Blessed is the man who walks not in the counsel of the ungodly, nor stands in the path of sinners, nor sits in the seat of the scornful; but his delight is in the law of the Lord, and in His law he meditates day and night" (Psalm 1:1). The Adversary deceived many of our brothers in humanity and makes most of them ungodly and scornful in their lives. The world became full of such naïve people, who are negatively influenced by the enemy. We allow low-energy thoughts and deeds because we are disconnected from God, who is the only source of our spiritual strength. Then we are submerged into the world. However, God says, "... I will strengthen you, yes, I will help you, I will uphold you with My righteous right hand" (Isaiah 41:10). Meditation brings us to how we charge our minds with high-quality thoughts. To disconnect ourselves from the world, we need to sit with ourselves. We need to shut down our way of communications with the world, such as cell phone, social media, or television. Meditation on God's words is a great deal of wisdom that makes one regain that inspiration, hope, and positive attitude.

(3) Origin of Meditation in the Bible

Meditation is using the power of language by repeating a particular spiritual quote and consciously hearing that quote, which ingrains it into our mind, eventually becoming our nature. The hearing aspect originates from the Scripture, "Faith comes by hearing, and hearing by the word of God" (Romans 10:17). So hearing the word of God promotes faith. The repeating aspect comes from the Scripture "This I recall to my mind, therefore I have hope" (Lamentations 3:21). Watch the verb "recall" and what deep implications it carries. The verb emphasizes the meaning of repeating and remembering, which in turn leads to believing and promoting hope. Recalling and repeating bring to our mind assurance. This is the power of affirmation. Assurance by repeating a quote commands a man's subconscious and releases its enormous power of faith. Meditation feeds the subconscious mind, which in turn accepts and then transmits these positives to the conscious, causing us to align to our God-intended nature.

King David repeated many sentences in the Psalms. "I have set the Lord always before me; because He is at my right hand I shall not be moved" (Psalm 16:8). "Those who trust in the Lord are like Mount Zion, which cannot be moved, but abides forever" (Psalm 125:1). The character of David depicts a man who was not moved by facing troubles; a man not moved by all the challenges he met in his life; a man who was responsible for God's people. Throughout his Psalms we see that David found out he could strengthen himself by repeating scriptural statements over and over; statements that annulled whatever opposition came his way. David repeated many statements that annulled his fear as well. "The Lord is my light and my salvation; whom shall I fear? The Lord is the strength of my life; of whom shall I be afraid?" (Psalm 27:1). A man with no fear is one who relies on the name of God and can defeat Goliath (1 Samuel 17:45-48). In the name of God, in the name of Jesus Christ, we can defeat any obstacle in our lives.

If meditation on God's word is the method used by the Psalmist to overcome all challenges and to be a successful king, we are in need of the same method. God manifested to him that meditation promotes faith, and through faith we can move mountains. We are in need to use the same method to face the challenges in our lives. This method has proven successful with many in the Bible, and it can be successful with us too.

(4) Meditation and the Subconscious Mind

Many of us have found this paradox. We listen to a sermon in the church or via media about love or forgiveness, then we have a hard time applying these concepts in real life. Not only this, but the devil deceived some of us that these ideal concepts are only in books and are too hard to live in real life. The solution for this paradox is found in the function of the conscious mind comparing to the subconscious mind. The conscious mind is the receiver of information. It perceives the surroundings, which includes time, date, locations, and events. It functions through the senses. Its functions are associated with short-term memory. The conscious mind has intermittent activity that we call sleeping and waking. The subconscious mind is the sender of actions and reactions, some of which come voluntarily and others involuntarily. Its function is associated with long-term memory. The subconscious mind functions continuously. Its activity is twenty-four hours a day.

The subconscious mind is subject to the conscious mind. That is why it is called subconscious or subjective.[3] The subconscious mind takes orders from the conscious mind and acts upon those. The subconscious mind does not question the information received. It simply receives, reflects and reacts what it receives from the conscious mind. However, the subconscious mind does function by habitual thinking, not by just mere transient thoughts.

So most of us, once we hear a beautiful sermon of kindness or forgiveness, think that we've got it. Then we think that we will be kind and forgiving. However, when it comes to the real application, we find ourselves still far from kindness or forgiveness. The paradox is solved. We received these concepts by our conscious mind; however, these are not yet transferred to the subconscious mind from where we actually become kind and forgiving persons.

The explanation of the function of the subconscious mind is magnificently explained in the Bible. The Lord says, "If you love Me, keep My commandments" (John 14:15). The function of keeping is pertinent to the subconscious mind. When we keep God's commandments, then we will be forgiving and kind. King Solomon understood the sending function of the subconscious mind and stated in the book of Proverbs, "Keep your heart with all diligence, for out of it spring the issues of life" (Proverbs 4:23). The actual function of the physical heart is to continuously pump blood to the various parts of the body. However, the heart in this Scripture context signifies the subconscious mind. The verb *spring* signifies the sending aspects of the subconscious mind. We need to be cautious of our positive and negative thoughts, which in turn affect our emotions and behaviors. We need to entertain only positive thoughts. To do so, we need to read the Bible every day until we absorb it by our subconscious mind, until all our actions and reactions come voluntarily and involuntarily according to God's will. Paul the Apostle says, "Finally, brethren, whatever things are true, whatever things are noble, whatever things are just, whatever things are pure, whatever things are lovely, whatever things are of good report, if there is any virtue and if there is anything praiseworthy—meditate on these things" (Philippians 4:8).

(5) Experiencing the Power of God by Meditating on the Power of God.

Lack of spiritual knowledge is a source of pain and misery for all humankind. Lack of spiritual knowledge or ignorance in mind is the root of a weak spirit. As the Lord says, "Are you not therefore mistaken, because you do not know the Scriptures nor the power of God?" (Mark 12:24). When we know the Scripture, we know the power of God. When we meditate on the power of God, we will experience the power of God and we will have a strong spirit. Lack of spiritual knowledge also leads to worldly desires, complaint and material attachment. Worldly matters are just glimpses which disappear as a mirage. If we would like to experience God and His power in our lives we must enrich our minds with spiritual knowledge and Divine principles. If we would like to know God, we have to know the Holy Bible. When you know your God, you will not find yourself interested in anything else. The mere reading of the Bible not only eliminates the lack of spiritual knowledge, but also builds within that great interest of recognizing the amazing characteristics that God bestowed on humankind. Spiritual knowledge is a journey that starts with reading the Bible. Reading the Bible for one time makes us know that there are spiritual laws. Abiding in reading the Bible makes us to memorize these spiritual laws. The perfect results come by applying these laws in our lives. Applying these laws in our lives brings us to ultimate true happiness and genuine wisdom. The ultimate spiritual knowledge is pure knowing of God. Reading the Holy Bible and the saints' commentaries lead us to discover the way for contemplation and spiritual advancement. "... the gospel of Christ, for it is the power of God to salvation for everyone who believes" (Romans 1:16).

We may say that we do not have resources for spiritual knowledge; we do not have a Bible or books. Simply like that, buy a Bible and books. You can get a free Bible shipped to your house from any church or any Christian organization. Why do we buy fertilizers for our grass and we do not buy fertilizers for our minds? We can find good books in garage sales; I found most of my valuable books in garage sales. Most of the time I take a book for twenty-five cents; sometimes they are free. Maybe we say we've never done that before! If it is something good, learn to do it. "Learn to do good" (Isaiah 1:17).

(6) Necessity of Clear Conscience so Meditation Works

Clarity of thought, purity of heart, stability of emotions, and harmony of behavior come by the dwelling of the Holy Spirit in us, who will teach us everything. As Jesus says, "But the Helper, the Holy Spirit, whom the Father will send in My name, He will teach you all things, and bring to your remembrance all things that I said to you" (John 14:26). Sons and daughters of God are guided by the Holy Spirit in every aspect of their lives, not only in big decisions, but also every trivial subject on a daily basis. Literally, the Holy Spirit will teach us everything that we need.

However, before the Holy Spirit tells us what to do and how to act and react, we have to have a clear conscience so that He can guide us. Without a clear conscience, our perception of His guidance will not be clear. The essence of self-improvement and spiritual advancement is following the direction of the Holy Spirit. The essence of the guidance of the Holy Spirit starts with confessing our sins. When we confess our sins, God will cleanse us. It is God's promise, "If we confess our sins, He is faithful and just to forgive us our sins and to cleanse us from all unrighteousness" (1 John 1:9). Once we confess our sins, God will forgive and forget the past. Once we are clean from all of these, we are in place at the beginning of the right track of self-improvement and spiritual advancement, which all in turn lead to the pure knowledge of God.

Meditation ingrains God's words in our mind; hence, the Holy Spirit is joyful within us, and He will empower us to clear ourselves from sinful acts. By meditation, we are giving room inside us to God; we are freeing ourselves from the preoccupation of unnecessary mental and spiritual burdens. The more we are free within our heart, the more the Spirit of God will fill us.

When the meditation is firmly perfected by regular practice, and when we attain a pure conscience, and when our spirits become strong because of union with God, and when we gain firm faith, our words come from a pure spirit, and they become so positive and effective. The man who reaches that level has mostly mastered silence. He does not even have a desire to speak. As in, "He who has knowledge spares his words, and a man of understanding is of a calm spirit" (Proverbs 17:27). The source of his knowledge is God; the secret of his calmness is the spiritual union with God. For that man silence is equated with wisdom. His mind is always thinking and meditating on God. He is full of God; his mind is saturated with the power of God. When he speaks, he speaks slowly with a low, warm tone. All his words are full of wisdom and sweet like honey. All his words are full of positives, hope, healing, and medicine to the soul and the spirit.

Forgiveness is another important step before meditation. When we forgive someone, we never mention his faults anymore. If we still mention his faults, we still did not forgive him yet. As God says, "For I will forgive their iniquity, and their sin I will remember no more" (Jeremiah 31:34). Forgiveness is a commandment of God; it is fundamental and conditional. "For if you forgive men their trespasses, your heavenly Father will also forgive you. But if you do not forgive men their trespasses, neither will your Father forgive your trespasses" (Matthew 6:14-15). Simply like that, by forgiving others, you are positioning yourself so that your sins can be forgiven by the Heavenly Father. Forgiveness is a direct result of the release of a man from his ego; a profound factor leading to a peaceful mind and healthy body. If you feel that you are sin free and heaven is granted, do not forgive. However, you cannot be a heaven grantee if you still don't know how to forgive. No one can reach the ultimate potential of his mind without forgiveness, peacefulness and calmness in mind and body. Consequently, the direct result will be a harmony between the mind and the body. Meditation brings to a man's mind all of forgiveness, peacefulness, and calmness.

Another important step before meditation is asking God for remission for any sin. It is a terrible thing to live in fear; sin is the worst fear. As much as we ask God for remission, we have to bless any person who has hurt us in the past. By this, we get rid of obstacles hindering the mind from meditation.

(7) Meditation and Goals Determination

We set up our ideals according to spiritual standards. We decide on our goals according to God's will and to our own ability. Our first goal should be glorifying God in our lives. The second goal is to make sure of our eternity at every single moment of our lives. The fundamental rule of setting up a goal is that it be according to God's will and according to our abilities. Meditation helps us to discover the will of God and how much actually is our ability. God created us to reach such goals for His purpose. However, we have to be careful that, though there may be a lot of noble goals, they may not be according to His will. King David wanted to build the temple, a noble goal, but that was not according to God's will. When we do God's will in our life, we will do it in its proper time, and He will equip us to do it. Successful people are those who know the will of God in their lives and do it.

Meditation helps us to focus on the goals and the means of our goals. There is always a way when there is a will. However, goals do not justify means. Meditation provides us with clarity of mind, which in turn helps us to set goals and recognize how to accomplish them. Some of us were able to set up goals, but not all of us were able to reach them. Meditation provides us with the can-do mentality, which is one of the fundamental needs of reaching a goal. Once you have a clear mind and can-do mentality, you can have your goals crystalized. Then you need to write them down so you do not forget. After you determine your goals and have clear vision about them, you need to make a priority list for which goal will come first. Then you need to count the steps from where you are and your goal. Avoid any unnecessary steps that will distract you from your goals. Also consider continually asking yourself, "What am I doing to match my goals? This way, you keep yourself on track. When we accomplish our goals and fulfill our destinies, we have magnificent joy. As the Bible says, "A desire accomplished is sweet to the soul" (Proverbs 13:19).

3: Meditation Is a Helpful Tool for Healing and Good Health

(1) Meditation Goals

There are many goals for meditation. Spiritual awareness, peace of mind, physical healing, and developing one's character are some of the most important ones. There are many types of meditations; each type can help achieve a different goal. In spiritual awareness, meditation awakens man to realize that God lives within. When we have a spiritual awareness, we will have peace of mind. When we have peace of mind, we will attain spiritual healing. And then, the spiritual healing manifests itself in physical healing. Although all goals of meditation are important, physical healing is the tangible goal for many of us who are faced by serious illness. Physical healing happens when we meditate on God's miraculous power of healing and bring this power to the afflicted part of the body.

Meditation also helps us to develop our personality and character to improve our self. When meditation is perfected by continuous active practice, the spirit becomes strong, the mind becomes focused, and the body becomes healthy. The spirit becomes strong because of the direct rapport with God, the Spring of all strength. As a result, the mind is focused, which in turn can discern and choose what is positive and reject what is negative. When the mind is focused, we can have a peaceful state of silence, and in that silence we realize who we are. In that peaceful silence, we can recognize ourselves and can discover our true character. When we know ourselves, we know our destiny. Meditation inspires man to reach a natural state of a clear mind, pure heart, and Divine connectedness.

(2) Meditation as Therapy for Stress and Negative Emotions

Most of us may have started to practice meditation to get help with physical illness, to reduce mental stress, and to achieve peace of mind. In many cases it is those who are faced with hardships and life-threatening illness that find the solution in meditation. The longest way to God is man's mind; the shortest way to God is man's heart. The mind is always impatient and occupied with countless negative thoughts day after day. By soothing our minds, we allow fostering the word of God and let our souls be connected to Him, then faith is promoted. When faith is strengthened through meditation, we can experience God's power of healing.

Meditation is a magnificent tool to reduce stress for those who suffer serious illness. Those who cope with a diagnosis of life-threatening illness and the side effects of treatment can have stressful lives. Stress can often interfere with sleep, and sleep time becomes a session for bouncing negative thoughts about the fate and prognosis of that illness. As meditation reduces the anxiety and stress of the related illness, it improves the quality of sleep, and hence helps resume or improve the previous quality of life prior to the diagnosis. In some situations, meditation can keep the quality of life in a steady state. Once a man is faced with a certain diagnosis, whirlwind events occur starting with doctors' appointments, hospital admissions, financial burdens, and treatment. Sometimes treatment that is thought to be a cure can be worse than a disease itself. Meditation can improve secondary symptoms that are due to the primary diagnosis. For example, a man faced with a heart condition started to have stress because of this condition. The results were that he needed medication for the heart diagnosis and medication for the stress. As meditation helps to relieve stress, he may need treatment for only one condition.

(3) Meditation Promotes Faith

Meditation focuses us to control what we are thinking of, which in turn becomes what we deeply contemplate. We can surely experience God's healing by contemplating on His power of healing. The more we meditate on the power of God, the more the power of God will manifest in our lives. Continuous contemplating on the things we want to receive will make a link between these things and us until they become reality. We have to conceive things from inner faith to receive them for the outer Divine purpose.

When we have zero doubt, when we have absolute faith, and when we have complete comprehension that God is the Absolute Source of healing power, and that we are created by God, we can receive this healing at any moment. We need to remember that absolute faith is like a mustard seed, "If you have faith as a mustard seed, you will say to this mountain, 'Move from here to there,' and it will move; and nothing will be impossible for you" (Matthew 17:20). The mountain can be an illness, addiction, unforgiveness, obesity, financial hardship, smoking, marital failure, negative attitude, depression, fear, or lack of achievement. Meditation promotes faith, which is the key for the desired condition, hence the inevitable healing and restoring of our normal Divine state. As Paul the Apostle says, "Now faith is the substance of things hoped for, the evidence of things not seen" (Hebrews 11:1).

Faith promoted by meditation is based on two vital components: affirmation and visualization. Affirmation is a positive statement that depicts a goal that is hoped for. This goal can be healing or overcoming a hardship. Repeating affirmations by the conscious mind many times will press these statements into the subconscious mind where a lasting positive effect will occur.

The house of faith in a man is his subconscious mind. Reciting the positive affirmation must be with conviction until healing by faith is a matter of fact. Affirmation of faith is like the transcription that writes our healing from inside. And then the reward of this inner conception is to see the result confirmed from outside. An example of this could be a man practicing meditation to develop his faith, and he feels in his inner depth that he got healed. Then he goes to the doctor and test results confirm that healing has occurred. Visualization is another component of faith energized by meditation. Visualization is the capability to see these hoped for conditions as if they are already happening. Visualization-driven meditation causes the meditator to hold this hoped for image in his mind until he sees it in reality. Visualization depends on man's mind of imagination. The more detailed imagination a man can create in his mind, the more successful results will be. Meditation energizes this great power that God bestowed on every one of us, that is the powerful gift of imagination. God clearly boosted the power of imagination in Abram, when He asked him to count the stars, "'Look now toward heaven, and count the stars if you are able to number them.' And He said to him, 'So shall your descendants be.'" (Genesis 15:5).

(4) Meditation Promotes Healing

The following is my testimony of the work of God in my life. Healing through meditation is the most tremendous evidence of the power of meditation. The following are techniques I applied to get cured and stabilized from a heart condition, in medical terminology called cardiomyopathy, by using the magnificent power of meditation to achieve a tangible effect. It is important and vital to emphasize that this power of meditation is available to everyone, literally everyone, who is able to recognize and diligently seek this power of healing.

Meditation Is a Helpful Tool for Healing and Good Health

Based on all the observation and analysis that I came across throughout my life, I would like to categorize illnesses from the healing perspective. Then we will be able to know the use of the power of meditation. First: there is an illness that God will heal miraculously. As an example of this type of healing, Christ healed the blind man as in Mark 10: 46–52. The role of meditation in this type is to boost a man's faith to receive the healing from God. The blind man did not know what meditation was, but he kept asking with persistence and perseverance, which is a fundamental aspect of meditation. Second: there is an illness that God will heal; however, He will do so indirectly through using the vessels of physicians, pharmacists, and nurses. For an example of this, a man receives an operation and he gets cured. God used the healthcare team to heal this man. The role of meditation in this type is sustaining the man to not have a recurrence or relapse, and live a stable life. Third: an illness that God will give grace to bear. This illness could be the sharing of man in Christ's suffering. It is God's incomprehensible wisdom to sustain such a man for his salvation. An example of this type is what Paul the Apostle experienced. And the Lord answered him, "My grace is sufficient for you, for My strength is made perfect in weakness" (2 Corinthians 12:9). The role of meditation is trusting God and recognizing His grace, which in turn will make a man able to bear his illness.

Twenty years ago, when I was challenged by a heart condition, I did not know what meditation was. Also, I did not know why I was facing this condition since there was no family history nor was there a pre-existing condition. Because of my medical background, I knew that a heart afflicted with PVC-induced cardiomyopathy (PVC = Premature Ventricular Contractions) and an ejection fraction of 25% has a tough prognosis. This prognosis suggests that either I would need another heart, or in a few years I would be in the other life that is heaven. I tried to find a meditation to promote my faith and to receive that miraculous healing. Because of the severity of the medical condition, the available and known treatment was through a medical procedure. Facing the unknown made the situation challenging for me. I did receive the procedure to treat excess, uncontrolled beats in my heart. I knew, however, that this condition could come back. If science and medicine sometimes cannot determine underlying reasons for these extra beats, they are labeled *of unknown causes*, and there may be no known reasons for a recurrence.

After receiving a successful procedure, I decided to help myself with meditation. I read countless articles about different types of mediation, until I came to develop my own meditation, a meditation on the name of the Lord Jesus Christ. My meditation was based on using the power of language by repeating a particular inspiring biblical statement, and hearing that statement, which would boost my faith until it became true in my life. As mentioned before, the hearing factor comes from the biblical Scripture, "Faith comes by hearing, and hearing by the word of God" (Romans 10: 17). The repeating factor comes from the biblical Scripture, "This I recall to my mind, therefore I have hope" (Lamentations 3:21). As I practiced my meditation on recalling and repeating, I brought to my mind assurance. This assurance by repeating an inspiring phrase commanded my subconscious and released its enormous power laid there. This power is God's given gift to every man. So, I developed my inspirational quote that is, "In the name of Jesus Christ I am healed." The answer for why I used the name of Jesus Christ in affirmation is found in these Scriptures, "If you ask anything in My name, I will do It" (John 14:14). "Whoever calls on the name of the Lord shall be saved" (Joel 2:32).

Striving for surviving and not to face any recurrence, I obtained a model plastic heart, and kept reciting another statement, "In Christ, my heart is beating regularly." I dedicated focused attention to this activity on a daily basis. I used this plastic heart as a tangible object to keep focusing during meditation. Moreover, I used the power of imagination. I used to imagine that these electric foci that cause the uncontrolled beats as points of ink spotted on my heart and my heart was in a flask of glass. In my imagination, I poured out water and this water washed away these spots. At my three month post-op visit, which coincided with three months of practicing my meditation, the doctor told me that my heart was getting better, that my ejection fraction was 55%, which is fairly normal. So in my mind, I realized that the meditation was helping me. In other words, I was helping my heart with mediation in the name of the Lord Jesus Christ.

Now after twenty years and looking back at the general picture of what happened, a union of the power of faith and the power of imagination met in the practice of meditation with the net result being steady health all these years. Faith is gained by meditating on God's word. Meditating on God's word is achieved by autosuggesting to myself certain statements that unlock God's healing from within. It is ironic but most sad that when one is faced with a prognosis, he keeps contemplating on the negative prognosis while he wants healing. We reap what we sow (Galatians 6:7). You can reap healing when you sow faith in Christ. Contemplating on the negative prognosis establishes it until it does become reality. It is magnificent when one can see the sun behind the cloud. It is amazing that one can inspire himself by declaring certain biblical verses and positive statements that boost his mental and spiritual state to break through the prognosis, allowing healing to become reality. This is called autosuggestion. *Indeed, autosuggestion is an instrument which we possess when we are born.*[4] When man knows that the power of faith is laid deep in his subconscious mind and this faith is unlocked through autosuggesting healing biblical verses, he becomes conscious of how to receive Divine healing. Then through God's grace, he can be receptive to God's will to restore physical health and spiritual strength.

I believe that meditation boosted my hope to be bigger than my pain and my illness. I believe that meditation energized me with a strong spirit, which in turn did not allow the weakness of my heart to pull me down. I believe that meditation can help every one of us. I believe that these previous lines will help many as a breakthrough for those who believe and are willing to help themselves through meditation. The Lord is good to those who trust in Him. Meditation did not boost my hope only, but also my willpower. After surviving many challenges associated with my illness, I found myself writing this poem:

Even though my illness drags me to go under the ground,
I will not let my will to go down to the ground.
As long as I am on the ground,
I am going to reach my destiny and add another
victory on the ground.
So, one day when I go down to my ground,
People will remember what I did when I was on the ground.

Even though my illness drags me to fall behind,
My hope will keep pushing me from behind.
And as long as Christ is helping me and He is always around,
I will achieve my goals with focused mind.
So, when my story goes around,
People will be inspired and reach their destinies with
willpower all aligned.

4: Comprehensive Meditation and Affirmations

(1) The Comprehensive Meditation

What meditation will provide us with a complete, fulfilling life? There are many meditations that can help each person to fulfill a certain goal. However, there is a need for a meditation that is not just to provide a means of coping with life, but to live a life as Christ wants us to live. Christ want us to live the life of purity, the life of faith, the life free from fear. He wants us to love one another. Christ wants us to be humble, living in obedience and thanksgiving. As a result of humbleness, He will bestow on us wisdom. As a result of wisdom, we will be able to have self-control. As a result of self-control, a man will focus and direct his life to what is good.

A comprehensive meditation is one based on complete spiritual principles, which will be reflected in all aspects of life. It is the meditation that puts a man's being in sacred rapport with God and in harmony with God and himself. The sacred rapport with God is one of the vital pillars for an ultimate meditation. Through His grace, we are able to live a successful, joyous life. Harmony is the direct result of the comprehensive meditation - harmony of the spirit, mind, and body as God primarily created man. Connectedness with God provides a strong spirit. A strong spirit directs the mind to be focused. A focused mind welcomes and fosters positive thoughts, which in turn reflect in a healthy body.

(2) Affirmations to Overcome Negative Thoughts

To have a life changing meditation, there is a need for powerful affirmation. An affirmation is a positive proclamation that by repetition takes root in the subconscious mind. There the change will start to take place. The results appear in actions, reactions, attitude, and behavior. The repetition inspires us to believe until we see the positive change in reality. The repetition has to be on a regular basis. The affirmations have to be recited with patience and endurance until the change happens. The passionate repetition is the reprograming of our minds.

Every man is exposed to countless negative thoughts on a daily basis. These thoughts are pushed onto our human race by the devil. Some of us are conscious of this mind-battle, and some are not. Meditation makes us conscious of these negative thoughts. Christ will never push a thought of fear or anxiety onto man. Positive affirmations annul the effects of these negative thoughts. Not only this, but also it acts as a firewall around our mind that prevents any penetration of negative thoughts to our minds. The honest, fervent repetition uproots the negative seeds that were unknowingly planted in our minds. And then after a time of meditation, we begin to think, speak, act and react in ways synonymous to those affirmations. Hence, after the continuous practice of meditation, we see it acts as a seal guard to our minds so that nothing negative can be thrown into our minds again.

(3) Self-examination and Affirmations

Before writing an affirmation, we need to find out what behavior, action, or reaction that we need to change. We need to conduct a self-examination and be specific in our findings. This is the process of identifying what we need to change in ourselves. Self-examination is conducted through questions. These questions will address behavior, motivation, and the inner being. This is the first step of a man to know himself. The answers to the questions of the examination will begin the collection of information and insight for knowing oneself. Once we know ourselves, we can work on ourselves for a journey of endless self-improvement through meditation and affirmation. The journey of self-improvement is sparked and sustained by the grace of God.

The first and foremost question is, where are we from Christ? In chapter one, we discussed that God is Omnipresent and He is in supreme control. Christ is the Sole Source of strength, peace, and wisdom. These are all needed for joyous life. So by finding where are we from Christ, we are finding where we are from these components of a joyous life. The core principles of self-examination are stated by Paul the Apostle, "Examine your-selves as to whether you are in the faith. Test yourselves. Do you not know yourselves, that Jesus Christ is in you?" (2 Corinthians 13:5). The following are some of the most important questions a Christian needs to address while he is spiritually examining himself. Do I see myself as a child of God? Do I act, react, and live up to this concept? Do I recognize God's love in my life? Do I have peace in Christ? Do I follow God's commandments? Do I have purity of thoughts? Do I have faith? Do I love God and His creation? Am I obedient? Do I live the life of thanksgiving? Am I humble? Am I wise? Am I focused on God, family, career? Do I have patience? Do I have a positive personality? Am I accurate in what I do? Am I an optimistic person? Do I have hope? Do I have willpower to change my life? Am I calm person? Am I confident of God's love and that everything will work for good in my life? Am I a gentle person? Do I have compassion and mercy? Am I a forgiving person? Am I a godly, prosperous person? Am I a kind, and cheerful, giving person? Do I provide comfort and sympathy to those in need? Do I provide spiritual healing to those desperate for it through presenting to them Christ and the Bible? Am I a source of the solution to problems? Do I overcome any negative habit dominating my life by an evil spirit? Am I overcoming myself and being renewed through Christ? If the answer to any of the previous questions is no, I am not this type of person, or I need to be this person, then there a need for an affirmation to inspire this trait in our lives.

(4) Effective Affirmations

Why are some affirmations effective and bring excellent results? Why are some affirmations not making any effect in a man's life? There are certain criteria for affirmations to be effective. When these criteria are fulfilled, and the reciting of affirmations becomes a habit through the practice of meditation, positive outcomes become inevitable.

Positive: As the change that is hoped for to happen through meditation is positive, the affirmation needs to be positive as well. When we are writing an affirmation, we need to remember the purpose of this affirmation. Writing an affirmation is fundamental to writing a code to program the subconscious mind. Do we need to program our minds by something positive or negative? Of course, positive. So an affirmation must be positive. The critical point here is that most of us write affirmations to overcome negative traits, behaviors, or mindsets. Therefore it is vital that any negative mentality does not come into the affirmation or it will be a challenge getting rid of the negative aspect.

Personalized: It is I who wants to change myself through the grace of God, so the affirmation must be personalized. Everyone's affirmation will be different than another person's for certain goals to be achieved. Generalized affirmation may bring the hoped outcomes when we write and say it on a personal level. When the affirmation is personalized, it is tailored to the issues that the meditator wants to change. Personalized affirmation includes or starts with one of the following phrases: I am; I have. Despite this being true, there are common affirmations that can be used for everyone. Example: I am calm. Calmness is a great trait.

So if many people use this affirmation, they are taking a common affirmation and personalizing it for themselves.

Present tense: Writing and proclaiming an affirmation is to be in the present tense. Through repetition on a regular basis, the subconscious mind will receive the affirmation that is needed and work on it. If you need this positive change to happen, do you want it now or in the future? Certainly everyone wants the positive change to happen as early as possible. Even with the proclamation of change you want to see, the present tense is realistic. I eat healthy food versus I shall eat healthy food. I quit smoking versus I shall quit smoking. One of the most amazing affirmations stated in the present tense is what Paul the Apostle said, "I can do all things through Christ who strengthens me" (Philippians 4:13).

Short and simple: An affirmation must be a short phrase or statement. There are many reasons the affirmation is to be short and simple. Reciting a short affirmation is much easier than reciting a long affirmation. It more accessible to encode the subconscious mind with short affirmations versus long affirmations. Adding and associating all these factors together will harness the effects of affirmations, which in turn will make meditation bring tremendous positive outcomes. Easy to recite affirmations will be easy to repeat regularly. Short, simple affirmations will encode the subconscious mind, and hence will produce positive outcomes.

Specific: It is important to be specific in the affirmation. If the affirmation is to overcome procrastination, state in a concise way what you will be if you are not procrastinating. Example: I am proactive. When the code "I am proactive" is ingrained in the subconscious mind, a man will handle life matters without delay according to the needed timeline and their importance. Also, we need a specific affirmation for each trait that is hoped for.

Visualize: Visualizing and gaining what is hoped for is of faith. *Faith is to believe what you do not see; the reward of this faith is to see what you believe.*[5] It is highly recommended that an affirmation be accompanied with visualization. To achieve visualization, an affirmation needs to be reasonable. A reasonable affirmation will empower the meditator by the belief of achieving what is hoped for.

Whole well-being: There are three main components of every man. These are the spirit, the mind, and the body. There is a great need to address all these in writing affirmations. It is remarkable to work on the three components as a whole to promote well-being. It is ideal to work on the spirit to be strong and connected to God. When the spirit is strong and is in sacred rapport with God, His grace will guide us to have a focused mind. When we have a focused mind, we can focus on the health of the body.

(5) The Source of Affirmations

Positive affirmations are positive words that gradually will lead to a positive life, so the need is for words that bring life. The Bible is the word of life. The Lord Jesus Christ says, "It is the Spirit who gives life; the flesh profits nothing. The words that I speak to you are spirit, and they are life" (John 6:63). We are in need to use Christ's word as a source of affirmation as His words contain and impart life. As much as the affirmations are our part to do, it is the grace of God and the Holy Spirit that empower us to carry on these changes in our lives. As most of us turn to meditation to find a remedy for health issues, the word of God brings health to the afflicted. The secret of health is revealed in the book of Proverbs: "My son, give attention to my words; incline your ear to my sayings. Do not let them depart from your eyes; keep them in the midst of your heart; for they are life to those who find them, and health to all their flesh" (Proverbs 4:20-22). When we meditate on the word of God, we will have life and health. When our affirmation takes its source from the Bible, our meditation drives us to the spiritual growth and never-ending journey of knowing God. When we meditate on the Scripture, our lives reflect accordingly. As a result, we will change our habitual thinking. When we meditate on God's words, we obtain wisdom. When we have wisdom, we can process life with steady cautiousness away from the traps of the human adversary.

Every man faces two major temptations. One temptation comes from within. This is the desires of the flesh. Flesh desires war against the spirit, and the spirit wars against the flesh. The other temptations come from outside. These are presented to us by evil spirits. Both types of temptations are continuous. The winning over all these temptations starts from inside. When we win from inside, we win from outside. When we meditate on God's words, we are strengthening our spirits by the living power of His Spirit. As Paul the Apostle says, "For the word of God is living and powerful, and sharper than any two-edged sword, piercing even to the division of soul and spirit, and of joints and marrow, and is a discerner of the thoughts and intents of the heart" (Hebrews 4:12). When our spirits are strong, we can overcome the desires of the flesh. This is the true victory. When we overcomes ourselves, we overcome the world and all its temptations.

(6) Meditate on Christ

The successful, wise processing of life comes from taking heed of an ideal example, namely One who handles life wisely and has been successful. Christ is the ideal example for every man who wants to process his life in wisdom and become successful in all aspects of life. The Lord Jesus Christ says, "Take My yoke upon you and learn from Me, for I am gentle and lowly in heart, and you will find rest for your souls" (Matthew 11:29). The Lord teaches us to take His yoke, that is, to follow His commandments and take Him as a guide in our lives. As He becomes our guide, we learn from Him. We learn from Him all that He instructs us to do, and leave nothing out. When we meditate on Christ and His teachings, we ingrain His seeds in our subconscious minds. Afterward these seeds bring forth fruits. These fruits are our actions and reactions, which all come to resemble and be the expression of His living in us.

The secret of troubles in the world is imbedded in the envy and endless fighting of the Adversary against our human race. Unseen evil spirits are the underlying cause for divisions, divorce, illnesses, fear, hatred, anxiety, denying God, living in sin, rebellion, wars, cheating, dishonesty, depression, and despair. This is clearly stated by John the Apostle, "We know that we are of God, and the whole world lies under the sway of the wicked one" (1 John 5:19). Knowing and understanding that we are in continuous battle with these opponent spirits, we have immense need to live in Christ. Christ overcame the world and all that is therein. The Lord Jesus Christ says, "These things I have spoken to you, that in Me you may have peace. In the world you will have tribulation; but be of good cheer, I have overcome the world" (John 16:33). Our peace is in Christ. When we meditate on Christ, we can overcome the world. When we meditate on Christ, He within us will equip us to face the tribulation in the world. When we meditate on Christ, He will be in us and we in Him; hence, thereafter we can overcome the sway of the wicked one. The secret of overcoming all that is going on in the world lies in meditating on and living in Christ.

Obedience is another jewel of meditating on Christ. Disobedience was the first sin man fell into by listening to the devil and not following God's voice. God's voice was the first voice Adam and Eve heard in the garden. The second voice was the voice of the devil. As a result, the whole human race is in a continuous challenge with the second voice to disobey God. Some think they are wise and make their own rules. Some think that they are good. Their goodness is proclaimed by not hurting anyone, helping others, and always following policies and rules of made by men. Despite this goodness being great, obedience to God is the most marvelous thing a man can do. God's commandments are superior to man-made rules. Christ in His humbleness teaches us obedience to the Father, "For I have come down from heaven, not to do My own will, but the will of Him who sent Me" (John 6:38). When we meditate on Christ, obedience will be in our nature. And then each one can say to God, *Let me do Your will.* What we will to do and choose for ourselves may indeed be good. However, the will of God for us is the best.

Christ teaches us to seek the kingdom of heaven, "But seek first the kingdom of God and His righteousness, and all these things shall be added to you" (Matthew 6:33). However, the devil drives a man to seek the vanity of the world that perishes. Trusting in riches and big bank accounts is vanity. Pride of achieving an important title and career advancement is vanity. Loving possessions and racing for getting the most advanced technology is vanity. Spending life in pleasures is vanity. We all know that the world is passing away, "And the world is passing away, and the lust of it; but he who does the will of God abides forever" (1 John 2:17). *This is the greatest wisdom—to seek the kingdom of heaven through contempt of the world.*[6] Meditating on Christ brings us into the life of righteousness. Meditating on Christ will make us to live in the world, but the world not to live in us. When Christ becomes the center of our meditation, we will do the will of the Heavenly Father. The will of the Father is to seek His kingdom. Meditating on Christ guides us securely in this world until we reach the kingdom of heaven. The kingdom of heaven is the ultimate goal of every man living on earth. There is our eternal home with our Savior, the Lord Jesus Christ.

5: In Christ Meditation

(1) What is In Christ Meditation?

In Christ Meditation is a comprehensive meditation of affirmations based on the Bible and Christ's teachings. Some of these affirmations confirm the sacred rapport of Christ with His creations. Other affirmations are the direct result of the living Christ in us and the work of God's grace by the Holy Spirit. *In Christ Meditation* is the medication and remedy for a magnificent life, which the Lord wants us to live. It is an inclusive meditation that inspires the spirit, mind, and body. It is the meditation of which Christ and His teachings are the integral core of each affirmation. Paul the Apostle teaches us to focus on the Lord, "Looking unto Jesus, the author and finisher of our faith, who for the joy that was set before Him endured the cross, despising the shame, and has sat down at the right hand of the throne of God" (Hebrews 12:2). In these days more than ever, our human race is in desperate need to focus on Christ. When we focus and meditate on Christ, He empowers us over sins in which the devil always wants to entrap us. Through His grace, when we overcome sin and live in continual repentance, we can witness for Him. This witnessing will start by experiencing Christ in our lives and then our families and friends could see Him through our behavior and manners. When we contemplate on Christ, He will sustain us and will carry with us the cares of the current world.

We become what we meditate on.
What we meditate on becomes our essence.
When we meditate on Christ, Christ becomes our essence.
When we meditate on Christ, the grace of God changes us into Christ-like persons.

(2) In Christ Meditation

+ *In Christ, I Am a (son, daughter) of God. Christ lives in me and loves me. Christ is my Strength, Peace, and Salvation. Christ is greater than the world. I think what Christ would think, I say what Christ would say; I do what Christ wants me to do. Glory to God.*
  1. *In Christ, I Am Purity. I feel God; I feel Good.*
  2. *In Christ, I Am Love. I love God and His Creation.*
  3. *In Christ, I have Strong Faith. I trust God; I have no Fear.*
  4. *In Christ, I Am Humbleness and Thanksgiving. I Am Obedience.*
  5. *In Christ, I Am Wisdom and Discernment. I Am Silence.*
  6. *In Christ, I control my Thoughts and my Senses. I Am Focused.*
  7. *In Christ, I Am Patience, Perseverance, Positivity, and Persistence. I Am Accuracy and Understanding.*
+ *In Christ, I Am a (son, daughter) of God. Christ lives in me and loves me. Christ is my Strength, Peace, and Salvation. Christ is greater than the world. I think what Christ would think, I say what Christ would say; I do what Christ wants me to do. Glory to God.*
  1. *In Christ, I Am Optimism. I have Hope and Willpower.*
  2. *In Christ, I Am Calmness and Confidence. I Am Gentleness.*
  3. *In Christ, I Am Compassion and Forgiveness. I Am Mercy.*
  4. *In Christ, I Am Prosperity. I have Abundance. I Am Kindness.*
  5. *In Christ, I Am Comfort and Healing. I Am the Solution.*
  6. *In Christ, I Am Healthy and Wealthy. I have Strong Memory.*
  7. *In Christ, I overcome illnesses and spirits. I overcome myself. I Am a new (man, woman). I Am Christ-like.*
+ *In Christ, I Am a (son, daughter) of God. Christ lives in me and loves me. Christ is my Strength, Peace, and Salvation. Christ is greater than the world. I think what Christ would think, I say what Christ would say; I do what Christ wants me to do. Glory to God.*

Two unique aspects to be considered about the *In Christ Meditation.* First: the main principle of the meditation is that God is the Whole Source of everything and we are His sons and daughters. As God's name is I AM, the meditation will include "I Am" with the letter "A" capitalized to emphasize our unique identity as His sons and daughters. Second: God is the Absolute Source of purity, love, wisdom, patience, optimism, and all the other merits of the meditation. If God is patience and we are His sons and daughters, we are patience. However, we are patience in relation to God. We are extensions of God's patience on earth. When we are *one* with the spiritual principle that we are meditating on, we can live it. Hence, we can provide it. This means that my essence is purity, love, wisdom, patience, optimism, and all the other principles of the meditation. Once we understand and believe that these spiritual principles are our nature that originated from our Heavenly Father, these will be ingrained in our minds and we can live them.

How are these affirmations formulated? What are the Biblical verses that are the foundations for each affirmation included in the *In Christ Meditation*? Why do we need to meditate on these spiritual principles in particular? The answers to these questions are the topics of the following parts of this manuscript.

(3) In Christ

It is simple to say that the *In Christ Meditation* will start with In Christ. However, there are deeper principles that imply this very beginning. The Lord teaches us that we need Him in every aspect of our lives, "For without Me you can do nothing" (John 15:5). Without Christ we are lost and astray in the turmoil of the world. Without Him, we are facing the world and the human Adversary alone. It is to no avail facing the world on our own. Christ is the Creator and the Source of life; He is the breath of every man. He is the vine and we are the branches. Can a branch sustain itself without a vine? Certainly not. So we are. Paul the Apostle states that all things that God wants him to do, he can do through Christ. "I can do all things through Christ who strengthens me" (Philippians 4:13). When we process our lives through Christ, He will equip us to do it. The reason that some have been challenged by life and wanted to give up is that they did not get the help that they need from Christ. People do not seek help from Christ because they may think they are independent. This is one of the saddest traps of our society. This trap puts us into loneliness and depression. If everyone of us thinks of being independent, why do we need friends, parents, and families? *In Christ Meditation* is the medication for the nowadays trap called "I am independent."

The name of the Lord is the key that causes the Heavenly Father to accept our requests. "Whatever you ask the Father in My name He will give you" (John 16:23). When we go to the Father with the name of the Lord, the Son will direct us to ask for what is necessary for our lives. He will guide us to request according to His will. The name of Christ is the name of salvation; it is the name of blessing. There is no greater name than the name of Jesus Christ. It is vital to meditate on Christ by reciting His name at the beginning of each affirmation.

Man's ego has separated him from God. Ego and all its identification breaks the union between God and the human being, then the net results are confusion of mind and the loss of hope. One of the main reasons behind ego and its identification is the lack of spiritual knowledge. Ego brings pride; pride brings fall. God is inside us; God is inside you and me. He is inside everyone. God is inside everything. "For of Him and through Him and to Him are all things" (Romans 11:36). Submitting of one's ego brings a man to a pure knowledge of God. This leads into accepting God's will in his life. When we accept God's will, we understand the purpose of the Divine Wisdom behind difficulties we may encounter, instead of resisting and repining on them. This understanding will bring us into harmony with God. Only through this harmony can we really say, "Your will be done" (Matthew 6:10).

When the awakened mind focuses on Christ by meditation, man will recognize the living of God within. We will have a state of connectedness with God all the time. We will recognize our union with God through the Son. As we recite the name of Christ in meditation, we have mental communion with the Father. By this mental communion, our spirits come into realizing the union with God's Spirit. The practice of *In Christ Meditation* promotes understanding of the real meaning of the Omnipresent God and brings us into spiritual union with God. "But he who is joined to the Lord is one spirit with Him" (1 Corinthians 6:17). When the mind is enlightened with comprehensive spiritual knowledge, when it is alert and positive, it then can enter the state of spiritual union. When we comprehend this spiritual union, we will be able to live our lives as Christ wants us to. He will show the way of life. As the Psalmist says, "You will show me the path of life; in Your presence is fullness of joy" (Psalm 16:11). A life guided by Christ is a peaceful, fulfilling life no matter what the Adversary pushes in our way. When we meditate on Christ, we will recognize His presence in our lives, and then His presence will fill our lives with true joy, which everyone is looking for.

(4) In Christ, I Am a (son, daughter) of God

Knowing who we are identifies the solution for many issues of our lives. Not only to find the solutions, but this knowing can also be preventative for many problems. To know who we are, we need to address this vital question, *Who am I?* I am a spiritual being created by God. And only in Christ, I will go back to God. As we believe in Christ, we receive our right of sonship. The disciple

John states in his gospel, "But as many as received Him, to them He gave the right to become children of God, to those who believe in His name (John 1:12). In addition, every time a man says, "I am", he proclaims the name of the Creator, the Source of all human being, God. I AM is the name of God, "And God said to Moses, "I AM WHO I AM." And He said, "Thus you shall say to the children of Israel, 'I AM has sent me to you'" (Exodus 3:14).

Through meditation on our being sons and daughters of God, we inspire our minds to live accordingly. When we have the mental setting that we are sons of God, our way of handling life will be different. We are the sons and daughters of the Master of Life and the King of kings. The hidden and unseen reasons for many problems we face in these days are because we did not act according to this concept. A teenager asked his Sunday school teacher, "My class is going to have a party. Usually they smoke and drink. Should I go?" The teacher was skilled and paused for few minutes then replied, "You are a son of God." Then he asked, "Will these behaviors match with a son of God?" "I got it," the youth replied.

Meditating and living as sons and daughters of God can be the remedy for divorce. One of the reasons of divorce is that children of God marry others who don't have the same beliefs. In the past, God has instructed His people against such marriage (Deuteronomy 7:3). There are two absolute conditions to accept a spouse: First and foremost, a spouse must have the same beliefs. To marry a spouse, he must be a son of God as you are daughter of God. No other choice. Paul the Apostle teaches, "Do not be unequally yoked together with unbelievers. For what fellowship has righteousness with lawlessness? And what communion has light with darkness?" (2 Corinthians 6:14). The second absolute condition to accept a spouse to yourself is the fear of the Lord. If a man or a woman fears the Lord, he will fear to cheat. He will fear to harm or do evil things that hurt himself, his spouse, and his marriage. The word "absolute" means there is no other way. It means do not override these conditions by any means. When a man fears the Lord, he will be humble and God will give wisdom for how to handle his marriage and how to relate to his spouse. "The fear of the Lord is the instruction of wisdom, and before honor is humility" (Proverbs 15:33). After fulfilling the first two absolute conditions, then look for a loving spirit and high morals. These principles no one can steal. These are pillars of a successful marriage. The one who fears the Lord will have all these pillars. They come as a package and are not divided. When you build your marriage on strong spiritual absolutes you are building your marriage on a concrete foundation, and the winds of the world cannot shake it.

A dear friend got engaged. As she kept knowing her fiancée more and more, she started to have doubt about her future marriage. Her mom recommended that she talk to me. After she stated the whole character she'd come to know about her fiancée, I recommended that she leave him. Knowing my friend is a strong believer and lives as a daughter of God, her fiancée's traits did not match her. As is the case of many nowadays, she was attracted by his life achievements and being successful in his career. "Is he in Christ? Will he go to the church with you every Sunday? Will he accompany you to the weekly Bible study? Will he raise your children in the fear of the Lord?" I asked. None of these questions got yes as an answer. So a few weeks later she left him. Two months later, she called me and stated that she had peace leaving that man. She is happy and her family is happy as well. She is trusting God that He will send her the right spouse at the right time, a man who will love her as himself (Ephesians 5:22-33). We need to know that not having peace and no family consensus are signs from God not to proceed with marriage. When we meditate on who we are in Christ, it will be more clear to recognize His voice. His voice and His signs will guide us to rightly process the issues of life.

(5) Christ lives in me and loves me

Christ lives in me and loves me is not just an affirmation abstracted from the Bible, it is a Divine promise of the Lord Himself. Jesus in His prayer to the Father says, "I in them, and You in Me; that they may be made perfect in one" (John 17:23). He is in you and me and everyone who believes in Him. The spiritual essence of God lives in me. This promise is in line with the right of sonship - *I Am a son of God.* I have His character in me. He is my very being. With this Divine promise, there is a condition for the continuation of this unity, "He who eats My flesh and drinks My blood abides in Me, and I in him" (John 6:56). This is the communion of a man with the Father through the Son. This is the most precious gift that God gave to the human race for our salvation, His Son. Paul the Apostle lived that way. "I have been crucified with Christ; it is no longer I who live, but Christ lives in me; and the life which I now live in the flesh I live by faith in the Son of God, who loved me and gave Himself for me" (Galatians 2:20). Through meditation that promotes faith, we can perceive the living of Christ in us.

While this Divine promise is true and recognized by many, the human Adversary has succeeded in influencing some of us not to live according to this principle. In some communities, the devil succeeded to make us think it is humbleness to say, "I am a sinner." This has a tremendous undesirable effect on the subconscious mind. It is an incomprehensible concept to state this about oneself. This has a negative effect which actually influences a man to live in sin. Christ died for us while we were sinners, that through Him we will overcome sin and iniquities. If we say that no one can live righteously, we state that our Christ's redemption is in vain. If I am in Christ, it is then scriptural to state I am repentant, not a sinner. This has a positive and constructive effect on our intellect. This means I recognize that in the past I have sinned, but now I am in Christ and live in repentance. We are human and susceptible to sin because of the continuous temptation of the Adversary. However, in Christ we can live in awareness of and persistent cautiousness against the traps of the devil. Even if a man is overtaken by a sin, let him repent, confess his sin, and partake of the communion to abide in Christ. Meditation on the Divine promise, *Christ lives in me and loves me*, makes us live in continual repentance.

In a previous work location, a coworker wanted to test my limits. After some time, he realized that I have tolerance to all his deeds. Usually in these situations, a smile and silence are my greatest tools to react. While these tools are used in the work place, prayer is my asset at home to resolve issues. So, after some time this colleague questioned my silence and my conservative reactions. "Are these reactions a kind of silent hate?" he asked. "I cannot hate you, nor judge you, not even not forgive you. Christ lives in me; I cannot do anything of these that makes me not feel the presence of Christ in my life. I cannot afford losing Christ," I replied. We can change the way we live and the way we handle resistance and oppositions by changing the way we think. When we think of the living of Christ in us, we will act and react positively because we have direct help from Christ.

The need of ingraining Christ's love in our subconscious appears in hardships, serious illnesses, and when things do not go well. Losing trust in God is one of the meanest temptations a man may encounter. It is the beginning of serious downward spiraling consequences from which some of us do not recover. Usually this happens when things go as we do not expect, when we are faced by difficulties, and when we mistakenly think that our prayers are not heard. And then, the Adversary plays his mean role, "How is it that God loves you?" The devil comes to those who are facing hardships and says, "I do not think God loves you since you have this trouble in your life." Through the affirmation, *Christ lives in me and loves me*, we are settling in our minds a firm concept of God's infinite love. God has unconditional love for you and me. Christ has sacrificed His blood for our salvation. There is no greater love than this (John 15:13). As Christ sacrificed His blood for our sake, we ought not doubt His love, neither that He will withhold any good thing from us. Meditation on His love strengthens our faith and puts it into practice. Soon enough these hardships will pass and become anchors of strength.

(6) Christ is my Strength, Peace, and Salvation

Time is the only factor in life that no one can store nor retrieve. Energy is the fuel for man's strength. Our strength is a reflection of how much energy we have in our system. The more energy we have the more strength we express in our day to day activities. The ironic and most interesting thing is that every one of us wants more energy, which directly affects our strength. However, we waste what we have. We waste our energies in gossip, social media, negative emotions. We waste our energies by allowing the Adversary to seed in our mind thoughts that do not match with Christ. Hence after, we experience a whirlpool of events that we don't even want to manifest in our lives.

When we meditate on Christ by the affirmation – *Christ is my Strength, Peace and Salvation*, we are aligning ourselves with the Sole Source of energy. The beauty of this principle is in recognizing the Divine resource of energy is a source of peace. When a man knows that he has the energy and strength to perform the tasks on his daily agenda, he has peace. There is a direct relationship between energy and peace. Having energy gives us peace that we will accomplish what we need to do. With peace, we can conserve our energies. The core of having both strength and peace is our mind staying focused on the Lord, "You will keep him in perfect peace, whose mind is stayed on You, because he trusts in You. Trust in the Lord forever, For in YAH, the Lord, is everlasting strength" (Isaiah 26:3-4). Meditation is the medication for staying focused on the Lord, who is the Sole Source of peace and strength. The Psalmist realized this treasure of strength, "God is our refuge and strength, a very present help in trouble" (Psalm 46:1). In addition, by focusing on Christ, He will guide us to how to use our strength wisely.

Peace is the state of harmony of man with God, himself, and his surroundings. When we have peace with God, we have peace with ourselves, and hence we have peace with all our surroundings. There is no peace in the world nowadays because the human Adversary causes conflict between man and God. The direct results are that man has neither peace with himself nor his family, friends, or co-workers. The agony and distress in the world will be resolved by restoring the peace of man with God. Meditating on Christ as our peace is the vital remedy for the turmoil in the world. If Christ is our peace, nothing in the world will be able to shake us. When we perceive the peace of Christ, we can convey this peace into the world. Through meditation, we can live in the peace of Christ that surpasses all our minds, and can spread this peace to the world. When meditation on peace becomes an established practice in our lives, conveying peace to the world will be a one-way direction. We bestow peace to the world, but the turmoil of the world cannot get into our minds.

Salvation is by God's grace and not by man's work. Salvation includes deliverance from troubles and destruction. Salvation includes the overcoming of day to day worries and concerns. Most of us have the concept that salvation is applied only for the forgiveness of sin. Truly, salvation is for forgiveness of sin and the release from the bondage that it brings. Yet it is important to know salvation as an ongoing process of life. We need Christ's salvation from our day to day cares and anxieties. We need Christ's salvation for the intolerance, agony, and unrest that fills the world. Through affirmation, when we establish in our minds that Christ is our salvation, the grace of God delivers us from the turbulence of the world. King David had seen what we see as well, but his power in overcoming all these challenges is that he recited, "He only is my rock and my salvation; He is my defense; I shall not be moved" (Psalm 62:6). When we meditate on Christ as He is, the essence of our strength, peace and salvation, nothing in the world can move us.

(7) Christ is Greater than the World

It is a simple fact that God is greater than the world. In accurate realization of the nature of God, He fills the whole universe. His presence fills the heavens and above the heavens, the earth and below it, the sea and its depth. God is omnipresent. However, in hardships we may forget this fact. The devil puts a dark cloud on the eyes of those who are in distress and makes them think that their problems are greater than Christ. As a result, some lose hope. Some doubt their faith. Some try to solve their problems by embracing more problems. Our problems will come to an end when we realize this fact from within, "You are of God, little children, and have overcome them, because He who is in you is greater than he who is in the world" (1 John 4:4). We are sons and daughters of God. Christ lives in us. He is greater than any problem, any hardship, any force, any project, and any business. Christ is greater than the world and what is in the world. In Christ, the Divine help that we are looking for on the outside is within in us. No one has gone to Him for help who did not get solutions for his problems. The Lord Himself teaches us to go to Him in troubles and He will give us rest. There is no problem without a solution except for those which are not submitted to Christ. As a matter of fact, for those who realize that Christ lives in them and who take Him as their guide, He guides them to avoid problems through wisdom and prudence.

(8) I think what Christ would think

One of the ultimate goals of meditating on Christ is to think like Christ. Only when we meditate on Christ's teachings, will we train our minds to think like Him. This training is an ongoing process and every day activity. Thinking like Christ develops by asking ourselves, "If Christ were here, would He think this way?" To excel in this thinking training process, we need to ask ourselves this question in every matter. Some of us may think we need to ask ourselves this question only in big matters that require life-changing decisions. We feel we can handle small life matters on our own. However, Paul the Apostle says, "... bringing every thought into captivity to the obedience of Christ" (2 Corinthians 10:5). We need to bring every thought into the obedience of Christ. Christ explains His thoughts plainly in the Bible. Only through understanding, keeping, and applying the Scriptures, will we be able to think like Christ. Only through practice can we take our minds from the earthly matters to the heavenly realm. When the practice of thinking like Christ is perfected, we can fulfill what Paul says, "We have the mind of Christ" (1 Corinthians 2:16).

When we think like Christ, we will see life with a whole different view. We will not judge a woman standing at the corner of the street to be picked up for whoever can pay. Christ did not judge the adulterous woman, why should we? We will see this woman simply as deceived; one who yielded by her free will herself to the Adversary. As a result, the devil took over her mind to act this way. Thinking like Christ makes us see the thief as a naïve person, who did not know that Christ can provide. If he knew that simple fact, he wouldn't steal. When we attain Christ-like thinking, we will see that we all are like branches on the tree called humanity. We all came from God and we all want to go to the Father at the end. However, the enemy wants to steal us from our Father and make us go astray. When we think like Christ, you and I will see every man as a good man because he is the creation of the Father, even those who behave badly. They are good men, but they are deceived by the Adversary to behave this way. When we see a person acting in sin, we can through gaining the glorious mind of Christ, instead of condemning them, look at them with Christ's eyes of redemption. By thinking like Christ, we will inspire them through our actions and reactions to be conscious of their deeds; hence after, the grace of God can release them from the devil. And then, they will think and act like Christ wants them to. When we think like Christ, we will think of love, peace, purity, patience, forgiveness, kindness, truth, wisdom, and mercy.

(9) I say what Christ would say

I say what Christ would say is the result of thinking like Christ. Words are the product of the thoughts. If we think like Christ, we will speak like Christ. To train ourselves in this path, we need to ask ourselves how Christ will speak? Will He speak gossip? Will He speak idle words? Of course, not! Why are we wasting a great deal of time and energy every day in gossip and idle words? One of the reasons for the contention and conflict between people is that they say words without considering their impression on the hearer. Words are windows for the hearts. By our words, we can build or we can destroy. Paul the Apostle says, "Let no corrupt word proceed out of your mouth, but what is good for necessary edification, that it may impart grace to the hearers" (Ephesians 4:29). We need to train ourselves to speak like Christ. In His modesty, Christ says to the Samaritan woman, "You have well said,

'I have no husband'" (John 4:17). He did not judge her nor make her feel bad. He gently drove her to believe in Him and gave her the living water. Gentle words will edify the hearer and will give comfort to the speaker that he spoke rightly.

Imitating Christ in His way of speaking, makes us abstain from idle gossip that removes the guard from the tongue. If we will give an account of every idle word that we speak (Matthew 12:36), we ought to refrain from gossip and talking vainly without purpose. If Christ is here, will He speak of earthly matters? Will He gossip? Will He speak with no purpose? Will He speak to ridicule others? If the answer is no, we ought to behave in the same way. In like manner, spiritual talk could be needed to edify one another. *Devout conversation on spiritual matters is a great aid to spiritual progress, especially when persons of the same mind and spirit associate together in God.*[7]

When we meditate on Christ in our thoughts, our tongue will know how to give the right answers at the right time. When we focus our minds on Christ, He will give us input for when to speak and when to be silent. As we are in a continuous confrontation with the Adversary, we need to ponder how to give tender answers to those who are pushed in our way by the devil. Solomon the Wise says, "A soft answer turns away wrath, but a harsh word stirs up anger" (Proverbs 15:1). There is too much anguish among people because people don't know how to give tender answers. It takes good effort to train ourselves how to provide soft answers.

(10) I do what Christ wants me to do

The root of each action is a thought. When our thoughts are in harmony with Christ, our actions will be in harmony with Christ as well. *I do what Christ wants me to do* is the affirmation that inspires a man to the ultimate noble level of processing life. At the highest level of meditating on Christ we will inevitably recite the Scriptures in front of temptations. This is the secret of winning over every enticement. Christ did so, and we ought to do so as well. Christ gave us an example of how we should deal with life, "For I have given you an example, that you should do as I have done to you" (John 13:15). A great deal of life is resisting the devil and his deeds. Keeping and proclaiming the word of God is the greatest defense against the devil. When we meditate on Christ, we will recognize the devil's thoughts and have spiritual power and stamina to resist him. All of us face great temptations every day. The longer a man postpones resisting the devil, the weaker he becomes. As a result, the Adversary eagerly takes full control of that man's mind and actions. Those, who by patience and longsuffering resist the Adversary, gain full power and victory over temptations. Only those who are able to resist the devil at the Christ-like level of thoughts have actions that are Christ-like.

A business man called me seeking advice on whether or not he should sue a previous partner. As the conversation carried on, it became evident that this business man knew his partner was not a godly man. Still, he had entered into this partnership. "Will Christ do this? Will He sue someone?" I asked. "I got the answer. Thank you! That is enough," he replied.

Most of us, maybe all of us, get challenged at one point or another by the issues of life. Then one of these questions arises, What should I do? Who can give the right direction? Which career I should pursue? Who is the good spouse for me that is the true gift from God? Should I start this business or go to school and have more education? Any of these are important matters, and one inappropriate choice can turn life to unwanted consequences. One aspect of absolute wisdom is to know what Christ wants you to do in your life and you do it. It is great prudence to seek God's will before approaching things in your life. The Lord says, "Counsel is mine, and sound wisdom" (Proverbs 8:14). So we can ask Him what we should do in any subject of life. What career we should choose. What spouse to marry. What house we should buy. What car to buy. When we do so, God says, "I will instruct you in the way you should go" (Psalm 32:8). When we know what we are to do, we can say, "I can do all things through Christ who strengthens me" (Philippians 4:13). From these verses, we can understand that the words of God are the secret to knowing His will. *I do what Christ wants me to do* is the affirmation that sets our minds to a higher level of understanding. In addition to meditation, we can seek God's will through prayer and fasting. The true green light of His approval is inner peace and the proceeding of things smoothly. If you don't have this inner peace, do not proceed. Wait for His peace.

(11) Glory to God

The glory of God is the direct and indirect goal of every man who lives in Christ's teachings. As God is the essence of our beings, we ought to live for His glory, "Therefore, whether you eat or drink, or whatever you do, do all to the glory of God" (1 Corinthians 10:31). Glory to God, He gave a developer the ability to build beautiful houses, and other men the ability to afford these houses. Glory to God, He joins a man and woman in marriage to have joy, to conceive and multiply, and to see the fruit of their work. Glory to God, He gave a man accuracy to design and invent machines that provide plenty. Glory to God, He gave man the ability to invent submarines as He created under the sea creatures. Glory to God, He gave man the power to develop airplanes as He creates birds to fly high in the sky. Glory to God, He holds the earth's orbit and the seasons. When we glorify God in our meditation, our eyes can see His glory in the universe, and then we glorify God in our actions and reactions.

Paul the Apostle summarizes it all and says, "Imitate me, just as I also imitate Christ" (1 Corinthians 11:1). When we think, speak, and act like Christ, the grace of God is conforming us into noble persons like Christ. We can present Christ to the world. We can present the light of Christ to the world. He is glorified in us when people see our deeds and glorify our Father (Matthew 5:16).

6: In Christ, I Am Purity. I feel God; I feel Good.

(1) Purity

Only through purity does man recognize the dwelling of God's Spirit in him. Only through purity is God's Spirit fervent and guides man's spirit. The power of man's spirit is sustained by the sacred rapport he has with God's Spirit. The strength of this sacred rapport is the fundamental root for the serenity of the mind, the strong will, and the health of the body.

God is Absolute purity. God's nature is purity. As sons and daughters of God, we are part of His purity. Purity is our being, and impurity is foreign to our nature. Purity is the original nature of our human race and impurity is the result of man surrendering his will to the devil. To recognize that purity is our essence, look at a child and his purity. A child in his purity trusts his dad and his mother. The purity of a child makes him forgive and forget what bothered him. The purity of children makes them enjoy gifts and events. The purity of a child is the reflection of the purity of God. As the children are pure, their prayers are heard by the Heavenly Father. Unless we become pure as children, we cannot recognize the presence of God within.

We need to live with purity to enjoy our life and God's given gifts. We need to restore that purity that was stolen from our human race by the Adversary through scheming and man's agreement. Through meditation on purity we can retrieve our primitive purity. The affirmation – *In Christ, I Am Purity* enables us to reestablish this purity. *In Christ, I Am Purity* awakens our being to be pure.

The motive of this affirmation is that we by our intention surround ourselves with a pure atmosphere. A pure atmosphere includes the selection of what is seen on television and what is read in electronic and printed material. The obsessions of sex, violence, and personal dominion are the devil's intention and are not of God. The thought that no one can live a life of purity is from the human Adversary. Meditation on purity is the medication for that thought. When we meditate on Christ as our being, we can live in purity and we can impart purity into the world.

When meditation on purity is perfected in practice and the affirmation *In Christ, I Am Purity* is rooted in the subconscious mind, purity is restored to man. It will come naturally to reject impure words and gossip. It will be our nature to convert from chatter to meditator. It will be voluntary and involuntary not to watch episodes that contain unclean scenes. Meditation is an excellent cleaning method of our minds and souls from the impurity of the world. We are sons and daughters of God. We can live in purity.

When we live in purity, we feel God, "Blessed are the pure in heart, for they shall see God" (Matthew 5:8). God is in every one of us. God is in you and in me. Through purity, we awake His presence from the back of the ship of our lives, as it were, and hence, He orders the storms to be still, "Then He arose and rebuked the wind, and said to the sea, 'Peace, be still!' And the wind ceased and there was a great calm" (Mark 4:39).

A few years ago, a healthcare professional called me to ask for information regarding one aspect of his business in which I have experience. After three minutes listening to this man, he expressed troubles in every aspect of his life, not only in the original intention for his call. The true help that I offered him is that I asked him to let God manage his life and then, only then, would He settle all the troubles he was facing. The man stated that this was well said, and he realized that all he truly needed was God in his life.

(2) Feeling God and Feeling Good

Not feeling good is synonymous with not feeling God. Our not feeling good is a main goal of the Adversary. Not feeling good can be the result of previous unwise behavior, spiritual warfare by the devil, or just a difficult day. Not feeling good can advance to such a high level until a man's soul is distressed. A tormented soul is a soul that lacks peace. Peace is the harmonious state that everyone everywhere is looking for. Oppression at work, fear about the future, regrets about the past, loss of beloved ones, disturbing dreams, despair of a better life, can cause the soul to be distressed. Not feeling good is a result of the impure clouds that the devil pushes on us to make us not to feel God. Most of us face these issues at certain points in our lives, and apart from Christ, we do not know what to do.

Meditation on the presence of God is the immediate tool to bring peace and tranquility to the tormented soul. *In Christ, I feel God* affirmation unveils the impure clouds that the devil pushes into our minds. Only when we feel the presence of God, will we feel good. God can restore the past and secure the future. God can heal all unwise behaviors of the past and lead us to have a bright future. Meditation on Christ is the great defense of the spirit that subdues the warfare of the Adversary. It lifts up a man's spirit above the troubles of the world. Reciting the affirmation – *In Christ, I feel God* reconnects us with God, who is at peace at all times. Once we are connected to and have rapport with God, we always have access to the Divine peace. This peace is available to everyone at all times as well. Once we feel the presence of God, nothing in the world can disturb us. As we, the sons and daughters of God, believe that Christ is our peace, we have immense peace that will overcome the tribulation of the world, and nothing can shake us.

A helpful tool to manifest the presence of God and restore feeling good is to recite Psalms. When we feel that we are anguished by the turmoil of the world, literally we need to sit in a quiet room and bring the Bible and meditate and recite Psalms until we feel God. The physical touch with the Bible is a tremendous source of feeling His presence. The vital key is to disconnect ourselves from the world, which means turn off cellphone and social media. If we need hope and counsel, recite Psalm 16. If you have a tough day and are looking for assurance, pray Psalm 20. Psalm 23 is wonderful for abundance and provision. If you are in a state of fear, Psalm 27 is a great defense. If you need the joy of trusting God, recite Psalm 34. Psalm 91 and 121 are powerful for protection and safety. The remembrance of past sins can be healed by reciting Psalm 32; repentance can be started with Psalm 51. Psalm 100 can express our thanksgiving to God for all His great deeds and mercy to us. If troubles are passed and we want to praise the Lord for His help, pray Psalm 146. Psalm 103 is a strong Scripture to bless God and to remember His benefits. Once we are in the position of peace again, we are in the position of power, and can face the world.

Purity begins by keeping the word of God. Then all spiritual advancement will follow in sequential manner. The word of God purifies man's consciousness. Then as a result of keeping God's word, we are pure. As we are pure, we feel the presence of God. As we feel God, we cannot but feel good. Thus, feeling God through obeying His word leads us to feeling good. We feel good as well because He forgives us our sins. It is by God's grace that we live in continual repentance and thereby continue feeling His presence. As we feel good because we're actually feeling God, we cause those who deal with us feel good as well. When I realized that feeling good and feeling God start from knowing the Bible, I found myself writing these lines:

Give me the Bible and leave me alone.
Come to see me,
You will not find me alone.
Since you left me, I am not alone,
I am never alone.
Since I was born, even before, I am not alone,
I am His own.
My God is with me,
I am never alone.
Give me the Bible and leave me alone,
I just want to be alone.
For when I am alone, I feel His presence in the being of my own.
Give me the Bible to meditate on God alone,
For when I meditate on Him and His Scriptures along,
Hope, peace and joy become my own.

7: In Christ, I Am Love. I love God and His Creation.

(1) Loving God

The essence of God is unconditional Love. The nature of I AM is endless Love. "God is love" (1 John 4:8). Through His love, the Lord Jesus Christ came to the world for our salvation. Through the Son, we are reconciled with the Heavenly Father. Through God's love, we receive the Holy Spirit. Through the Holy Spirit, the love of God is poured into our hearts and we proclaim Jesus Christ is Lord. Through Christ's love, we can pray to the Father, "Our Father in heaven" (Matthew 6:9). It is endless love. God is infinite love. Through His love, He sends to us mercy, "Through the Lord's mercies we are not consumed, because His compassions fail not" (Lamentations 3:22).

Since God is Love and I am His son, I am Love. You and I are Love. We are the manifestation of God's love in the world. We are part of the Whole love. God is the Whole love and we are part of His love. We are sons and daughters of Love. It is the absolute love of God to create us so we can have our being with Him. Through His love, He rejoices in us as children of Him, "Rejoicing in His inhabited world, and my delight was with the sons of men" (Proverbs 8:31).

In Christ, I Am Love is the most needed meditation to realize and to live God's love. *In Christ, I Am Love* is the affirmation necessary to manifest God's love in the world. The world is filled with hatred, anguish, and contention because we failed to recognize God's love and hence manifest His love to the world. As we recognize God's love, we will love God Himself.

However, the first and foremost action is to clean our hearts from the love of the world, evil passion, and earthly desires. *In order for you to really love the Lord, you have to completely empty your heart from any love that wrestles and competes with His love.*[8] *In Christ, I Am Love* is the tool for that sober action. The more we recite this affirmation, Christ will give us input to free ourselves from the world. The more our hearts are freed from the world, the more the love of God is manifested in our hearts. When God's love is manifested from within, it will be manifested in the external world and our surroundings.

When God's love is manifested in our hearts, we will find that we love our lives, our families, and our jobs. Through this love, we will find ourselves as passionate about the success and joy of others as about ourselves. Through this love, we will overlook peoples' mistakes and will avoid strife. The perfection of this love is to love those who mistreat us, pray for them and desire goodness for them. This love is characterized by patience; it is the love that unites families and friends. It is the love that succeeds and supersedes any human strife. It is God's love that is poured in our hearts.

(2) Loving His Creation

The solution for all problems in the world is love. Since God is love, then the solution to every problem is God. With God there is no solution that is impossible. Hatred is from the devil. Loving people is a part of our love to God. We can only offer what we have. We can provide love when the love of God fills our hearts. Once we recognize God's love in us and for us, it will be a matter of manifesting His love to all those around us. As we are sons and daughters of God, we need to express God's love to those who are deceived by the devil not to act with love. If there were no devil in the world, people would love each other and we all would live in peace. To love is to recognize God's love to us first; hence, we can express it to the world. When we meditate on the affirmation – *In Christ, I Am Love; I love God and His creation*, we begin to live in God's love and manifest it to others.

The toughest questions that we face are: How to love a spouse who does not help in the house or with the kids or with shopping or cleaning? How to love a spouse who is an addict and left the family? How to love a spouse who is controlling or does not separate between his or her role at work and being a spouse in the house? How to love a brother or a sister who would like to take over the family inheritance? How to love a daughter or a son who is gone astray against all morality and God's commandments? How to love your teenager who is aggressive in the house and does not respect the house rules? How to love the in-laws who feel that you took their son or their daughter from them or would like to be the decision makers in your home? How to love a family member who speaks mean words every time you encounter them? How to love a manager who overworks you and does not approve your vacations? How to love a co-worker who would like to show off as a hard worker and take credit for work not his own? How to love a co-worker who does not do his part nor go the extra mile to help out? How to love a business partner who would like to dissolve the partnership and keep the business for himself?

The Adversary influences us to talk about those who deal unkindly with us, making us forget an important commandment, that is to pray for such people. "But I say to you, love your enemies, bless those who curse you, do good to those who hate you, and pray for those who spitefully use you and persecute you" (Matthew 5:44). As a manifestation of God's love to those who have gone astray, we pray for them. When we pray for them, God will awaken them from the deception of the devil. When we meditate on Christ by the affirmation – *In Christ, I Am Love*, His loving character will manifest in our life. The ultimate Christ-like character a man can live is the loving character. The loving character is to love those who mistreat us with greater love than their hatred. This character of love always wins. The more we meditate on love, the more we foresee those people restored to the loving path by the grace of God, and the less we feel to talk about the negatives of them. The more we meditate on Christ, our loving character is strengthened, and through Christ-like character we see them as whole and perfect until this becomes reality.

A father called me complaining about his son who had dropped out of college, was smoking, and keeping ungodly company. After some time listening to the father, it was apparent that the father was busy working so much and not paying attention to his teenager who needed him. The father agreed to slow down, focus on his son, and pray hard that the Lord would restore his son. A few weeks passed and nothing happened. In another conversation, I asked the father to disperse holy water in the house, anoint the son with holy oil, and neither give advice to nor judge him. Also, every time the son would be going out or coming in, just say to him, "I love you, son. Christ loves you. The name of Jesus Christ be with you." The father and I prayed a few times together and we meditated on Christ's love. Two weeks later the father told me that his son had gotten a job and registered for classes. A few more weeks later, the mom called and stated that the son had quit smoking. The solution for our problems is love. It is not talking to others who have problems of their own and don't know how to deal with them. It is not judging those who've gone astray. The solution is to offer love.

When we love each other, we are fulfilling God's commandment, "You shall love your neighbor as yourself" (Mark 12:31). When we fulfill God's commandment, we will live in peace with one another. Every man is the creation of God; God created man in His image (Genesis 1:27). As we are sons and daughters of God, we can live in peace when dealing with others through the love of God. Meditation on God's love anchors us in His love.

To put meditation into practice, we need to be specific in our affirmation. *In Christ, I Am Love; I love God and His creation* – is a general statement that can be specific to bring love into effect for those deceived by the devil. Specific meditation can be as follows: *In Christ, I Am Love.* I love my son; my son is getting better. *In Christ, I Am Love.* I love my neighbor; I have peace with my neighbor. *In Christ, I Am Love.* I love my co-worker; my co-worker is very cooperative and has a team spirit. *In Christ, I Am Love.* I love my parents-in-law; we are a loving and harmonious family. When these specified loving affirmations take root in our subconscious minds, we will change our attitude toward them and our minds convey love to those whom we mention in our meditation. Then love, peace, and harmony are inevitable results.

Meditation on Christ is the work of ourselves on ourselves to manifest God's love. For meditation to work well, we need also to put other spiritual principles into practice. The following are some of these principles: 1) Pray for that person who is giving you a hard time. Our prayer will prepare us to receive Divine help to endure that person, and will help us to love him. 2) Recognize the real enemy is the human Adversary who wants all people to live in misery and in a state of division. There are many reasons that make a man behave badly. For instance, it could be either that he has a short temper, or he may be influenced by an evil spirit. Regardless the underlying cause of a person's bad behavior, through love we can see him as one who needs help. Whether he is a victim of an evil spirit or a victim of his own refusal to overcome his short temper, we need to deal with him in love. As we are loving persons and conscious of our deeds, it is our duty to provide for others Christ's love. And Christ will restore them. 3) Treat these people with love. This love will make them wake up from the influence of the devil. 4) Never complain about these people. The fact that we meditate on Christ's love and pray for those people makes us abstain from complaining. Complaining is a waste of time and brings more negative consequences. Meditation and prayer resolve hatred and bring positive outcomes. 5) Do not be bothered by the negatives that come from such people, and stay calm. One of the jewels of meditating on Christ is abiding in Christ's peace regardless of what is happening in the world or how others deal with us. Always remember, "Love never fails" (1 Corinthians 13:8). If you would like to live in peace, then live in love.

8: In Christ, I have Strong Faith. I trust God; I have no Fear.

(1) Strong Faith

Faith is the innate character of the true Christian believer. Once we realize that we are sons and daughters of God, we need to have faith in our Heavenly Father. Without this faith, we cannot delight God. "But without faith it is impossible to please Him, for he who comes to God must believe that He is, and that He is a rewarder of those who diligently seek Him" (Hebrews 11:6). We must believe that He is our Father and we are His offspring. He is our God. He is the Sole Source of life. As Paul the Apostle says, "For in Him we live and move and have our being" (Acts 17:28).

Because of the weakness of our humanity and the deception of the devil, some of us do not have faith. Some of us lost this key for fruitful spiritual life. The devil fights our human race with many vices; however, he focuses his fight using two major traps. These are the lack of faith and the loss of hope. Once a man loses faith in the Heavenly Father that He can provide and solve all his problems, that man can fall into despair. And when he falls into despair, he is prey for the Adversary. This is the condition of many of us nowadays. Meditation is the medication that boosts our faith. Through that faith, we realize the miracle that the weakness of man becomes strength and perfected through God's grace. Meditation is the tool that restores to us the fundamental principle of our sonship; that is, faith in God. Meditation is the remedy that helps us to regain faith. When we have faith in Christ, we will have what we need to proceed in our lives. *In Christ, I have Strong Faith* is the affirmation that unlocks faith within us. And when we have faith, we will realize that God can do for us more than we think or ask, "Now to Him who is able to do exceedingly abundantly above all that we ask or think, according to the power that works in us" (Ephesians 3:20). *In Christ, I have Strong Faith* is the tool that subdues doubts; hence after, faith flourishes by the power of the Holy Spirit in us.

When our faith is strengthened through affirmation, we will strongly believe that Christ can solve all our problems, for there is nothing impossible with Him. Most of us go around complaining about life. The mere fact that we complain about life makes us not able to enjoy life. Life is a gift from God. Complaining means that we are not happy with that gift. Complaining is another deception from the enemy. Most of the time we complain to people who sometimes do not have time to help us, or would like to help us but not up to our expectations, or who help us and ask a favor in return. Sometimes we complain to others who do not listen, then get offended that they did not listen to us. However, God is available to listen to us and He is the only One who can send to us the right help at the right time. It is amazing what the Shunammite woman did (2 Kings 4:8-37). She was in deep distress because her only son died in young age, but she complained only to Elisha, the prophet of God. She neither complained to her husband nor to the prophet's servant. The amazing part of this story is that when her husband asked her why she was going to the prophet, she said, "It is well." When the prophet's servant inquired about the state of her family, she said, "It is well." Great is the faith of this woman. Marvelous is the attitude of this lady. Learning from this great woman, faith inspires us not to complain, and if we do need to vent, it will be only to God. He is the only One who can help us.

Faith means God is my Father and will provide for my needs, "And my God shall supply all your need according to His riches in glory by Christ Jesus" (Philippians 4:19). We must realize that our needs are but one drop in God's endless supply of riches. God will let me know what education and career to pursue. He will give me the right job that fits my talents and, in that job, I will witness to Him and glorify His name. God will provide me with the faithful spouse and children. He will provide me with wisdom for how to process life. God will give me a house filled with love, peace, joy, and understanding. He will empower me to fulfill the destiny of my life. Meditation on Christ awakens our faith that because the Lord is our provider, He will indeed supply our needs.

Faith is the peace in the midst of the turmoil. Fear is the forgetting of the presence of God. God cannot be *not* existing in any fraction of time or in any place because God is omnipresent. God is the only Omnipresent Being; He fills the whole universe all the time, and is without beginning or end. So, fear is a matter of a transitory state of not comprehending the presence of God. Faith and fear are two matters that cannot exist in the same time. Either we have faith in God or we fear. The devil entrapped many of us to fear many things in life and to live in fear; hence, we do not fear God. If we fear the One, we will fear none else. Who is greater than God to fear? Faith annuls fear and allows us to perceive His Omnipresence. When we perceive God's infinite presence, we will trust that He will make all things to work for our good because we love and fear only Him. The fear of the Lord is to keep His commandments and not to transgress against Him. Anxiety and worry are forms of fear that result from forgetting our Father is with us. Anxiety depletes today's energy and does not solve tomorrow's problems. When faced with fear or worry, remember these verses: "Therefore do not worry about tomorrow, for tomorrow will worry about its own things. Sufficient for the day *is* its own trouble" (Matthew 6:34), and "Fear not, for I am with you; be not dismayed, for I am your God. I will strengthen you, yes, I will help you, I will uphold you with My righteous right hand" (Isaiah 41:10). As sons and daughters of God who follow His commandments, fear should not have place in our lives.

(2) Trusting God

Trusting God is to deeply believe that He is doing the best for us all the time, He is managing every step and every second of our lives, and He will provide us with the best. It means that we intensely believe that the Lord is leading our lives to victory, joy, and success. Trusting the Lord is to believe that He attentively listens to all our prayers and supplications. Trusting God means accepting "No" as an answer for some requests. It means that we confidently believe that He is able to provide us with more than what we think or ask.

A fifty-year-old engineer got laid off from the job he'd held for twenty years. The firm was in financial hardship. In a natural sense, it hurt him and the situation seemed cloudy because the economy was down when this happened. However, this man was trusting God. He believed that this must have happened for a reason. So, he accepted a job in the bakery department of a local grocery store. He stated to me that he loves to bake; maybe this is the time to pursue his hobby as a source of income. A few weeks later, a customer entered the bakery wanting special items for his daughter's birthday party. This customer was amazed by the talent of the enthusiastic baker and told him, "You must have been doing this for years." "Just for a few weeks," the smiling baker replied. The curiosity of the customer was stirred, and he asked, "What were you doing before?" As their conversation went on, it turned out that the customer was the owner of a firm looking for that particular engineer's talent. Through the grace of God, the engineer got that job and it was much better than his old job - better pay, better hours, better benefits. However, this is not the point. He was trusting God and never questioned His love for him.

Serious illnesses and hardships can be factors that shake one's trust in God and can propose doubt of God's love. We need to remember that hardships and difficulties are just turning points of life. All things happen for a reason; even something that seems bad at the time. And whatever challenge we may seek to overcome now, can be a source of blessing in the future.

The affirmation *I trust God* means I live by faith. This proclamation inspires one to be silent in the middle of tribulation. Being silent during hardships means that we put these hardships into the care of our Heavenly Father to do what is best for them. The book of Proverbs states, "Trust in the Lord with all your heart and lean not on your understanding" (Proverbs 3:5). This means always trust God not only in certain subjects or circumstances, but in all things and at all times. *I trust God* is the assertion that shifts our mental worry to tranquility; hence, we learn or come to understand God's ways.

(3) No fear

Fear entered into the world by man transgressing God's commandment. Before this first disobeying, there was no fear. Then after sinning, man started to experience fear. As a result of that fear, Adam hid himself from God and lost God's given dominion over the works of His hand (Psalm 8:6). Meditation brings us to true understanding of the fear of God. The fear of God is not to do evil, "The fear of the Lord is to hate evil; pride and arrogance and the evil way and the perverse mouth I hate" (Proverbs 8:13). Once we understand and abide in this fundamental concept that fearing God is abstaining from doing evil and following His commandments, He will pour out in us wisdom. "The fear of the Lord is the beginning of wisdom, and the knowledge of the Holy One is understanding" (Proverbs 9:10). By that wisdom, we will comprehend the unconditional love of God for His creation. Through that love, God sent Christ for our salvation. Now through meditation on Christ and the infinite love of God, we intentionally abide in His love. When we abide in His love, the first fear will take another form, that is caring not to hurt His feeling. Caring for our Heavenly Father's feeling is the ultimate form of fearing God. The affirmation *In Christ, I have Strong Faith. I trust God; I have no Fear* means I have faith that I will abide in God's love and will not transgress in respect of His feeling. I will not risk my salvation. Meditation on Christ brings us to abide in Christ and He will protect us not to sin anymore. And if because of my weak humanity I fall, through His mercy I will rise again and live in continual repentance.

The Adversary entices our human race with many fears. These are fear of death, fear of the future, fear of losing income and insurance, and fear of losing beloved ones. Meditating on Christ takes away fear. Christ is love and in love there is no fear, "There is no fear in love; but perfect love casts out fear, because fear involves torment" (1 John 4:18). Fear of death is the equivalent of fearing to travel to the Heavenly Father. The Christian principle is that earthly death is just being born into eternity, into the world where there is no pain or suffering. Death is the step to be in the presence of the Lord forever. Paul the Apostle annulled that fear for us by saying, "For to me, to live is Christ, and to die is gain. For I am hard-pressed between the two, having a desire to depart and be with Christ, which is far better" (Philippians 1: 21, 23).

Fear of the future is the fear of the unknown. With Christ there is no unknown. He is the Omniscient. He is managing every second and every step of our lives. Christ is in sovereign control of the past, the present and the future. God is here and everywhere. Since God is in the past and the present, He will be in the future. If God is in the future, why should we fear the future? Fear of losing income, job, a certain life style, and insurance is a form of worldly fear. Christ, not the job, is our source of income. Meditation on

In Christ, I have Strong Faith. I trust God; I have no Fear.

Christ brings to our minds the realization that He is our provision. The fears are traps of the devil to burden our minds, and hence we cannot focus on Christ. Meditation on Christ annuls these fears and clears our minds, which in turn leads to pure knowledge of God and who we are in Christ. *In Christ, I have Strong Faith, I trust God; I have no Fear* is the most needed affirmation. It brings us to be confident that God is our Father, our protector, our provider, and we have nothing to fear.

9: In Christ, I Am Humbleness and Thanksgiving. I Am Obedience.

(1) Humbleness

Humbleness is the mere realization of man to know that he without God is a son without a father. Humbleness is the understanding that we are the branches and Christ is the vine. As a branch cannot sustain itself by itself, we cannot sustain ourselves without Christ. Humbleness is the fundamental key for man to know himself. When we know ourselves, we can understand and advance in spiritual knowledge. If ignorance makes some to believe that they evolved from a monkey, humbleness inspires believers that they are sons and daughters of God.

Humbleness is the modest opinion of oneself. Regardless of how big the bank account or the sophisticated job or the high title, humbleness is the virtuous view of oneself. Knowledge and skills puff up, but humbleness is the understanding that these are just blessings from God. Humbleness protects one's skills and achievements. A man with pride may brag about his skills giving the enemy an opportunity to tempt him. Humbleness is the wisdom that makes man not to brag about his knowledge and skills; hence, these will ever increase and advance. Humbleness is from God. Pride is from the Adversary and is manifested as ego. Ego is the misconception that oneself is superior to others. It drives a man to haughty thoughts. It makes a man think he is superior because of what he has, what he owns, or what he does. Ego can become a huge obstacle to building relationships and achieving goals.

"Pride goes before destruction, and a haughty spirit before a fall" (Proverbs 16:18).

Many years ago during my education years, I got to know a man who boasted about the wealth and education of his dad. This fellow always talked about the very important job his dad held, and that he held this important job because of his education; the car that his dad drove; and so on. Despite the son's boasting, his dad had a great deal of wisdom and humbleness, but the son forgot to grasp this wisdom from his prudent father. In addition, this man forgot completely that not all of his friends had the same blessings as he did. Not all of them had an educated, wealthy dad. The result was that this fellow was not able to keep many friends, and he stumbled with his career.

Happy is the man who humbles himself to God. God will give him wisdom, and only with that wisdom man can rightly process life. It is vital that we examine ourselves. It is important to know at all times if we are humble or if pride has crept into our minds without our knowing. Arrogance is the most serious illness inflicted on our human race. Some have achieved a high education and are earning a secured living. However, because of pride they couldn't find their soul mates. God sent to those achievers their soul mates who are in the path of achievement, but arrogance caused those achievers to look only for their own choices not God's choices. The devil of pride held those achievers from sharing their blessings with others. The result is that those achievers are in loneliness and are discontent with life. Arrogance broke wonderful relationships. Some marriages ended in divorce because the man or woman was overtaken by the thought that he or she was better than their spouse. Moreover, pride led to separation and contention in families where parents were owners of family businesses in which the children worked. Some of these parents were influenced with pride, thinking they were the source of living for their children. Where the devil of pride is, there will be division and discontent. Where the acknowledgment of God is, there will be harmony and contentment.

In Christ, I Am Humbleness and Thanksgiving. I Am Obedience.

Meditation on Christ and humbleness brings man to reject his ego and the devil's temptation of pride. *In Christ, I Am Humbleness* is the remedy for pride. It is the affirmation that makes man to see himself with righteous eyes. Then he will not be distracted by earthly matters, and see himself as the reflection of Christ on earth. Christ is the Whole, Absolute humbleness; we are part of His humbleness. Meditation brings us to the remembrance that we are blessed by what we have achieved and what we have. Having a highly paid job and big bank account is only an expression of God's fairness, who rewards us for hard work. Meditation on humbleness helps us realize that we are all connected and in need of each other. Meditation on humbleness is the discipline of our ego to remember that all humans are branches in one tree called humanity, and all come from one Source, that is God.

(2) Thanksgiving

Humbleness is the twin of thanksgiving. Both traits function as cause and effect for each other. A humble man will be always thankful. A thankful man will be always humble. Christ inspires us to start everything with thanksgiving. Before He fed the five thousand, He looked to heaven and gave thanks. Before He raised Lazarus, Christ thanked the Father. Doing so, Christ instituted for us the life of thanksgiving. To live the life of thanksgiving, we need to count our blessings. We need to write them in a personal journal and have them handy. This list will be a great asset when temptations come our way. Knowing our blessings will be a great source of thanksgiving. This list will allow us to see what we have to be thankful for, and to not dwell on what is missing. When what is missing comes, we can then add it to that list. Then we find ourselves in an endless cycle of blessings and thanksgiving.

I know a man who got promoted to a new position in another department of the firm where he worked. Right before he moved from the first position, he got a raise. As with every promotion, there is an increase in the salary. In the new position, the income would be better than his previous income before the raise. That is why he accepted the transition; however, he pondered whether he should go on since now with the raise in the first position his salary would be higher. Even though the move was simply from one department to another within the same firm, because of budget constraints no adjustment could be made. That man decided not to think about the previous position as he is happy in the new one, and chose instead to thank God for the adjustment to happen. After a few months passed, he received a message from the leadership that a salary adjustment would be effective immediately. With that raise the new salary would be much higher than the previous income even with that raise.

As meditation practice is on a daily basis, the affirmation of *In Christ I Am Humbleness and Thanksgiving* will motivate us to thank God on a daily basis as well. To thank God, we need to slow down in our lives to see and recognize the immeasurable things to thank God for. We need to thank God that in Christ He covered us and still covers our sins. Imagine what our lives would be if all our sins and deeds were not covered by God's mercy. We need to thank God for reconciling us to Himself through Christ, the Intercessor of mankind. We need to thank God for sending Divine blessings every day on earth, even on those who deny His presence. We need to thank God for supporting us in our weak state, and helping us to go through hardships. Doing so will put the tempter to shame and cause him to flee from us. We need to thank God for our jobs and not to whine about them. We need to thank God for our children and not to complain about them. Being thankful will inspire us to know how to raise them in a godly manner. We need to thank God for having friends, family members, parents, or in-laws who live close by and are great help in times of need. Every day there are a lot of blessings that we need to thank God for. When we meditate on thanksgiving, we will see God's blessings. When we thank God for His blessings, these blessings will increase.

(3) Obedience

In addition to what was previously stated, obedience is a fundamental virtue to be a Christ-like person. Christ is the ideal example of obedience to our Heavenly Father. "For I have come down from heaven, not to do My own will, but the will of Him who sent Me" (John 6:38). Christ obeyed the Father all the way to the Cross for our redemption. As the Lord Jesus Christ is the perfect example of obedience, He also wants us to be obedient.

Meditation on obedience becomes an understood need when we recall that the disobedience of our father Adam was the origin of sin and the fall of all the human race (Genesis 3:7). Disobedience implies rebellion. Any rebellion is from the devil. From the beginning, the enemy stirs up man to rebel and disobey God and His words.

In these days, the deception of disobedience is taking another form; that is, knowing the words of God but not doing them. For example, most of us know the Lord's teaching is to forgive up to seventy times seven (Matthew 18:22). However, we see wonderful relationships broken because of lack of forgiveness, not even one time. Ironically, those who did not forgive may know the Lord's teaching, but in disobedience they did not forgive. The devil succeeded to frame this lack of obedience in the form of character or personality. Those who did not forgive might say something like: *I am a loving person, but I am done with my spouse; this is my personality.* Or, *I am a loyal person, but I am done with this friend-*

ship; this is my character. The enemy tempts those unforgiving persons to disobey God's words based on false perceptions of personality or character influenced by the culture. Obedience is following the word of God. There is a difference between knowing and doing. Obedience is doing what God's word tells us to do. When we obey God's words, they in turn will shape our personality into that of Christ's. When we have Christ-like characters, our behavior will be in accordance to the word of God.

On one level, obedience makes us friends with Christ, "You are My friends if you do whatever I command you" (John 15:14). On another level, Christ in His absolute humbleness raises us to be His family when we, like Him, do the will of the Father. "For whoever does the will of My Father in heaven is My brother and sister and mother" (Matthew 12:50). We will only be able to do the will of the Father when we obey His words.

In Christ, I Am Obedience is the crowning merit to be Christ-like. It is the completion for *I Am Humbleness and Thanksgiving.* A humble man will always be obedient to God's commandments. A humble man will be in thanksgiving to God for the promise that by obeying His commandments he will be safe from evil. "But whoever listens to me will dwell safely, and will be secure, without fear of evil" (Proverbs 1:33). The words of God are life and spirit; they are capable of changing our lives - when we obey them.

10: In Christ, I Am Wisdom and Discernment. I Am Silence.

(1) Wisdom

Wisdom comprises the principles to handle our lives with great care to reach the purpose of our lives. Wisdom is the accumulated knowledge and experience that enable a man to process his life with the least number of mistakes. There are many ways that we can get wisdom. The following are helpful tools to obtain wisdom:

1. Be humble. "When pride comes, then comes shame; but with the humble is wisdom" (Proverbs 11:2). Wisdom comes with humbleness. Seek to be humble and you will be wise.

2. Ask the Lord for wisdom. "If any of you lacks wisdom, let him ask of God, who gives to all liberally and without reproach, and it will be given to him" (James 1:5). It is important to know that no one has gone to the Lord and come away empty-handed. Didn't He say, *Ask and you shall be given*? Then let us ask God for wisdom.

3. Read about wisdom. Read the book of Proverbs again and again until you comprehend it, until you apply it, and until you become wise. Reading is a unique skill that enlightens a man's mind. It is very ironic that we want to get wisdom, but we do not want to read. We need to read and take heed. A man can write his seventy-year life experience in a book that we can read in seven days. How awesome is this? This reading will provide us with knowledge through another person's experience. Then we apply the wisdom we have read into our life. Doing this will add understanding to us in things we are experiencing, and gives us acquired experience of things that we were never exposed to. Then we take heed for our lives from that experience.

The devil held many of us in the trap of disliking reading. This trap has many faces. Some say, *I don't read because I fall asleep;* others say, *I get a headache.* The devil fights reading as he knows it is a source of wisdom for the human race. It is prudence to remember that reading is a source of light to man's mind. Also, it is very important to be selective in our reading. We need to read what will edify and help us.

4. Learn from your mistakes and from the mistakes of others. A wise man is he who never falls in one mistake two times. A wise man is the one who learns from what comes across his way. Often the devil can influence us to not learn from the mistakes of others by thoughts such as, *This doesn't happen with me,* or *This is not my business.*

5. Meditate on God's words. "I have more understanding than all my teachers, for Your testimonies are my meditation" (Psalm 119:99). The Psalmist David had wisdom because he consistently meditated on God's word.

The beginning of wisdom comes from the fear of the Lord. "The beginning of wisdom is the fear of the Lord, and the knowledge of the Holy One is understanding" (Proverbs 9:10). The conclusion of man's life is to fear the Lord and to follow His commandments. When we fear The One, we will fear no one. Who is greater than God that we could fear? "Let us hear the conclusion of the whole matter: Fear God and keep His commandments, for this is man's all. For God will bring every work into judgment, including every secret thing, whether good or evil" (Ecclesiastes 12:13-14).

As God loves every one, He is calling every one and is warning every one before troubles happen. Some of us are able to recognize God's voice. Sometimes some of us are influenced by the devil to do things and then repent with the excuse that God is merciful. Then when we do things against God, the same Adversary makes us fear and live in guilt. Sin is an offense to God, regardless how big or how small it is. In these days, the devil has succeeded in entrapping most of us to not fear God, and as a result we transgress against Him. The result is that we do not have intimate relationship with Him. In the meantime, we fear many things. We fear to lose jobs, insurance, business, houses, and social status. When we fear God, we will not fear anything else because who is bigger than God? The notable thing to know is that fearing God is the first step to obtain wisdom. Then through this wisdom, we will comprehend His love. Through wisdom we will understand that fearing the Lord is the principal wisdom for every man who would like to have a good life. Fearing the Lord brings safety for man. When you fear God, He sends His angels to be around you, keeping you safe (Psalm 34:7).

Absolute wisdom has three principles. First: know what God wants us to do in our lives and do it. God placed every one of us on earth for a purpose. Every one of us has an assignment to complete. When we do what God wants us to do, He will equip us for that mission. Noah's mission was to build an ark. Building an ark in those ancient days without advanced technology or tools could seem an impossible task. The only way Noah was able to complete his task is through God's help. God is willing to help everyone of us; however, every one of us needs to fulfill the purpose of his life. Second: be ready for our eternity in every single second of our lives. No one knows when the Lord will call his spirit from his body. If no one knows, then we need to be ready. In the afterlife there will be either heaven or hell. It is absolute wisdom to care about our lives and live in continual repentance so we pass to heaven. In a deeper meaning, it is absolute wisdom to seek the kingdom of God. Third: give a testimony why we believe in the Lord Jesus Christ, the Savior of the world. He came that we may have life. He loves us despite our sins and our mistakes. He loves us and sends His sun every day despite some of us rejecting

Him. How awesome is this love? This absolute wisdom is the ultimate wisdom to which everyone can aspire.

The affirmation *In Christ, I Am Wisdom* makes us channels for God's wisdom. The Lord is the Sole Source of all wisdom and knowledge, and He is willing to give wisdom to man. "For the Lord gives wisdom; from His mouth come knowledge and understanding" (Proverbs 2:6). Wisdom has many aspects: wisdom not to act rashly, wisdom not to believe all that we hear, wisdom not to repeat rumors, wisdom to trust the Lord, wisdom not to be wise in our own eyes, wisdom to set our eyes on heavenly matters while processing life with prudence, and wisdom to continuously read the Bible. Meditating on wisdom is the first step on the path of directing oneself in the way of wisdom. Meditation on wisdom is one of the greatest wisdoms a man can pursue. *In Christ, I Am Wisdom* is the perception of God's wisdom that makes us think, speak, and act as wise sons of God.

(2) Discernment

Discernment is the ability to perceive the conclusion of a matter. It is the ability to rightly evaluate subjects of life not according to the beginning but according to the end. Discernment is the just assessment of matters not according to the appearance but according to the core. Discernment is a twin of wisdom. A man of wisdom will know how to discern matters of life. With discernment, man will know what wisdom to pursue and possess. Most of us encounter matters of life the conclusions of which we cannot be certain. King Solomon says, "There is a way that seems right to a man, but its end is the way of death" (Proverbs 14:12). Only through discernment can man comprehend the end of a matter and not pursue ways that have terrible ends.

In Christ, I Am Wisdom and Discernment. I Am Silence.

Discernment is one of the most needed virtues when applying God's commandments. It is then, when we apply God's commandments, the devil fights our human race. It is wisdom and prudence to have discernment on how to apply each commandment. Applying God's commandments without carefulness can lead to unbearable consequences. There was a godly couple who always conducted their lives according to God's commandments. As they were wealthy and their children grown up, they opened their house to host newcomers to their city until they could settle. They hosted people who were introduced to them by relatives or friends from the church. They literally carried on the commandment: "Do not forget to entertain strangers, for by so doing some have unwittingly entertained angels" (Hebrews 13:2). One day they welcomed a college student who'd come to study at a university nearby. Despite the age difference between the wife and the student, the Adversary played his mean role as he had tried with Joseph and Potiphar's wife (Genesis 39). But this time the Adversary succeeded, and the conclusion was the divorce of the hosting couple.

It is great and honorable to apply God's commandments. However, applying His commandments without prudence can be used by the Adversary to cause us and our families to stumble. After unbearable consequences of applying God's commandments unthoughtfully, the Adversary may ask you, "Why did your God not protect you?" This mean temptation happens due to lack of discernment while applying God's commandments. Have mercy on yourself and seek God's guidance for how to apply His commandments with discernment.

In Christ, I Am Wisdom and Discernment inspires the two most important characteristics that man needs: wisdom and discernment. Through humbleness, the Lord gives wisdom. Through wisdom, man can discern life matters. *In Christ, I Am*

Wisdom and Discernment makes man receptive to God's wisdom. With that wisdom, we can discern life and do what Christ would do.

(3) Silence

Silence is deep wisdom. Wise people speak only when they need to speak and when their words will solve a problem or will add something constructive. Silence makes the fool appear wise. "Even a fool is counted wise when he holds his peace; when he shuts his lips, he is considered perceptive" (Proverbs 17:28). Silence is the ability to stay still in the middle of turmoil and hold one's peace. Then through silence and peace, man can reason, can face issues, can analyze, and can solve problems. However, no one can be silent all the time. We live in a world that encourages more verbal expression and communication. What is the solution then? Through discernment, a man knows when to speak and when to be silent. Silence is the third sibling of wisdom and discernment. Wisdom calls man to silence, and through silence meditation is perfected. Discernment calls man to know when to speak. When we speak, we need to speak as Christ would speak, we need to speak life. "Death and life are in the power of the tongue, and those who love it will eat its fruit" (Proverbs 18:21).

Christ has given us the most magnificent example of silence when He was facing the assembly of the high priest and the scribes. Even when the high priest asked Jesus, ""Do You answer nothing? What is it these men testify against You?" But Jesus kept silent" (Matthew 26:62–63). If we ever are faced with a matter of life and want to defend ourselves, we need to remember Christ's silence. When we meditate on Christ and His silence, He will defend us, "The Lord will fight for you, and you shall hold your peace" (Exodus 14:14). Most of us encounter circumstances where we feel urged to express ourselves and defend ourselves. Then our speech becomes an argument. Argument makes man lose his peace and there will never be a win. The act of arguing is not from wisdom. When an argument seems to be started, all we need is to practice silence and hold our peace. This is the great wisdom of children of God.

Silence despite speaking is a paradox and yet one of the jewels of meditation. In meetings or in socializing, silence can make people feel uncomfortable, so we find ourselves feeling we need to say something. On the other hand, wisdom calls for us sometimes to be silent. After many years of observations and practicing silence, we learn statements that can make people feel comfortable and we ourselves still keep silence. Examples of these statements: *I heard you; I understand;* or *I see what you are saying*. Such statements can be helpful when we encounter someone who would like to vent and we need to be reactive to what is said. Such statements help us to be in a state of silence, and through this silence we don't judge. As much as these statements make the speaker comfortable, it is important also to make him feel understood. Through wisdom and discernment, one can have a set of these statements as helpful tools for silence.

Silence is the remedy for saying words that we may regret later. Words last longer than a man's life. Those who hear our words will still remember them after we pass from this life. Words that come out of our mouth are not ours alone anymore. We will never regret what we did not say, as much as we regret what we have said.

Silence is the only trait that will never put us in shame. We are responsible for our words here on earth and in the Day of Judgment. The Lord says, "For every idle word men may speak, they will give account of it in the day of judgment. For by your words you will be justified, and by your words you will be condemned" (Matthew 12:36-37). Meditation on silence is the wisdom that makes us test and taste our words before we let them go out of our mouth. The affirmation – *In Christ, I Am Silence,* makes practicing silence become our nature.

11: In Christ, I control my Thoughts and my Senses. I Am Focused.

(1) Controlling Thoughts and Senses

A thought is the unseen seed that precedes every action. Senses are the entrances to man's mind. As living beings, our minds are continuously receiving thoughts and expressing thoughts. The nature of our human body is constantly perceiving the surroundings through our senses. Thought control is the fundamental way to great control over oneself; consequently, man will have the ability to lead his life to reach his goals. A man must determine for himself the following: Is my mind functioning for my favor? Is Christ the master of my mind? Am I using the full capacity of my mind? Am I discerning my thoughts coming from God or the Adversary? Am I selective in which thoughts I act upon? Do I tend to think with a positive attitude or with a negative attitude? Answering these questions is a powerful technique in controlling our thoughts and senses. Meditation is the essential tool for an excellent grip of senses and control of thoughts. Meditation on the word of God is the firewall that will gird up and protect our minds. "Therefore gird up the loins of your mind, be sober, and rest your hope fully upon the grace that is to be brought to you at the revelation of Jesus Christ" (1 Peter 1:13). The loins are the mental capabilities which are rooted in the power of thought. To gird up our mental abilities and be sober, we need to be conscious of our thoughts and alert to our senses. Meditation of thought control trains our minds with all its powers to be Christ-like.

While most of us mistakenly think that happiness is composed of self-pleasure and indulgence, genuine happiness is based on thought control and living a virtuous life.

Thought control is synonymous with self-control. True pleasure is in self-control with all its aspects. True pleasure is in reacting positively to peoples' negative actions and not allowing negative deeds of others to determine our actions or reactions. True pleasure is in learning from the past and not permitting our thoughts be held hostage to the regrets of the past. This self-control will cause man to focus on the present while planning for the future. True pleasure is in helping others and sharing God's blessings of knowledge, skills, and resources. True pleasure is in holding one's peace in the middle of turmoil. True pleasure is in silence when tempted towards a short temper. True pleasure is returning good for evil. True pleasure is in achieving the goals of our lives. As meditation is perfected in practice, man will find that happiness springs from within and does not depend on material possessions or external surroundings.

Thought control is longing for freedom from the dominion of worldly pleasures and desires. Freedom is misunderstood completely nowadays. Most people want to become free so they can do what they want. All that they want is driven by carnal desires. Carnal, fleshly and worldly, desires are against God. The real definition of freedom is to be free from sin and the bondage of carnal desires. The one who claims to be free believes in some particular standards and rules which articulate his life. We ask for our freedom to use it as a tool to reach our goals. To claim your freedom, claim to be free from carnal desires; something gained by thought control and the grace of the Holy Spirit. Meditation gradually programs our minds to ever-increasing high levels of thought control. We then have true freedom from futile thoughts that don't match our being sons of God.

Thought control is reflected in time control, energy control, and financial control. The devil has succeeded nowadays to deplete man's resources with the result that man lives defeated.

"Whoever has no rule over his own spirit is like a city broken down, without walls" (Proverbs 25:28). Social media and excessive socializing are common activities that deplete man's time and reflect poor time management. Gossip and sensual pleasure are the exact behaviors that drain man's energy and are aspects of lack of energy management. Over-shopping and buying whatever is wanted but not needed reflect lack of financial control.

The most common complaint we have in our day is the lack of time. *Where is the time?* or *I do not have time* are a question and a statement that circle with the breath of most. The lack of time is the most severe illness that has afflicted our generation. Causes of this illness are the social media, socializing, and TV. We spend time in front of social media with the hope it will lift up our mood, but the mood instead goes into a more depressed mode. We watch TV without knowing that we are programming our subconscious mind by what we see. Watching TV is the inviting of people whom we don't know into the middle of our houses and paying them money through the cable bill to take our time and money. The result is the loss of time as well as money, and more negativity. We socialize and escape socializing with ourselves. The result is feeling down because we do not face ourselves, and because we refuse to correct what does need correction in our lives. While many wonder about the lack of time, others are focused on their goals and achieve one goal after the other. Achievers have twenty-four hours just as all of us do. The only difference is that achievers have thought control that feeds into their time management. If we complain of the lack of time, we need to ask ourselves what do we do with the time that we have?

The mere complaining of lack of time is just wasting of time. The fact that some of us watch an event or episode on TV and don't like it yet talk about it for days is a huge waste of time. Some of us watch the same episode or movie over and over. Excessive socializing while one is overweight and there are addictive behaviors that need correction is a depiction of lack of self-control and a devastated life. It is a form of bondage. Meditation of thought control is the sparkle that awakens man's mind to take charge of his life. *In Christ, I control my Thoughts and my Senses* is the affirmation that brings renaissance to man's mental power. Meditation of thought control is the restoration of the function of the control tower that is man's mind. Practicing meditation is the start of mind control. As we are sons of God and we have the mind of Christ, by all means we are called to thought control; hence taking charge of all aspects of our lives. Only when we take charge of our lives and are being empowered by the grace of God, nothing of worldly behaviors and desires will have dominion over us.

Once man's mind is ignited for thought control and the value of time is pondered, man will value his energy as well. Most of us waste a great deal of energy as well as time in gossip, which can lead to judgment. However, the devil has succeeded in trapping the majority of our race in great wasting of energy through sensual pleasure. God has created intimacy so man can be fruitful and fill the earth (Genesis 1:28). God has created marriage for the expression of love between spouses. "Let the husband render to his wife the affection due her, and likewise also the wife to her husband" (1 Corinthians 7:3). Now with man's ignorance of God's spiritual principles, the devil can have dominion over him. For those who perceive marriage is for lust and exclude God from their mind, lust blocks their understanding and blinds their eyes. "… whose god is their belly, and whose glory is in their shame—who set their mind on earthly things" (Philippians 3:19). They live to fulfill their carnal pleasures. The devil has power over them. Satan has easily tempted our race because of the lack of self-control. "Do not deprive one another except with consent for a time, that you may give yourselves to fasting and prayer; and come together again so that Satan does not tempt you because of your lack of self-control" (1 Corinthians 7:5). As a result, man is driven into the remembrance of experienced enjoyment, which makes him yearning and desiring to repeat the same pleasure again and again. Then man becomes unknowingly mistaken between love and lust. Worldly lust does not provide any real joy, satisfaction, or contentment because it is both self-focused and temporal. Love is the greatest source of joy when it is right; love is the greatest source of pain when it is wrong. There is a complete difference between love and lust. If love is wrong, a man's mind does not get contentment even with repetitive pleasures.

The cultivation of mind by discipline and perfection of the various virtues results in the release of an abundance of energy, which in turn, leads to a supreme control over the senses. Afterward, disturbed emotions and confused movements of random thoughts will cease. Meditation empowers man to control the remembrance and the memory of pleasure and mistakes. The past has passed, but what do we plan to do in the future? Is the plan to repeat the same as what has passed? If pleasure of the past did not bring satisfaction and it affects the present, man needs to be careful with the present so not to waste the future. Meditation is the marvelous remedy for perfect control of physical energy. When physical energy is discreetly used and reserved, this energy is converted into spiritual energy that is used in meditation and prayers. When meditation is mastered in practice, an ever-increasing self-control is achieved. More thought control leads to more energy discretion, and more energy discretion leads to more self-control.

Thought control results in control of senses. Smell and taste are senses that need control nowadays. These can be controlled by fasting. Fasting is of the fundamental principles of the Lord's sermon on the mount (Matthew 6:16). The simple core of fasting is self-control, which is one of the fruits of the Spirit, and more importantly, obeying God. Moreover, the deeper concept of fasting is abstaining from one activity, eating, for a period of time, so we take time for prayer and spiritual practices which will nourish the spirit. As the devil deceived Adam, he still can deceive us to this day. Ironically, we put the fasting commandment aside and we eat thinking we're giving the body the required nutrition. However as a result, we may have obesity problems, diabetes, high cholesterol, and more important, our spirits become weak which leads to a disturbed mood and depression. We become like machines. We fill our stomachs then we look for how to use this energy. Some go to the gym for hours to burn calories they consumed in minutes, and some practice intimacy to take this energy out. Some go to the doctor to get pills to lower the extra pounds. Some are convinced that smoking is a great help to suppress their appetite and keep them in shape. Some have put themselves to surgery to decrease their stomach. Lord, have mercy! On the contrary those who fast and pray according to biblical teaching have good health and a strong spirit, and they never die from hunger.

In addition to what has been mentioned before about silence, self-control inspires man to have control over his speaking. We are in great need to know when we should calm our tongue and when we should talk. The secret of this control is bestowed in these verses: "In the multitude of words sin is not lacking, but he who restrains his lips is wise" (Proverbs 10:19). When you speak: "Let your speech always be with grace, seasoned with salt, that you may know how you ought to answer each one" (Colossians 4:6). With all our minds, we need to ponder this verse deeply, "Every idle word men may speak, they will give account of it in the day of judgment" (Matthew 12:36). How many idle words have we said? Dear reader, kindly pause here and check yourself. Practicing tongue control originates from the mind. The mind must reason, ponder, and anticipate the reaction of spoken words. A helpful technique in reasoning can be laid in these questions: Why should I say this? What is the benefit of saying this? Will my speaking add to or change the situation? Would Christ say this? Meditation on thought control and silence is medication for tranquility of the tongue. Hence the tongue is quiet, and man has time to listen, work, and achieve.

Meditation is the remedy for the lack of self-control. Lack of self-control makes the mind cloudy and not able to think clearly to analyze and reason. What would be the life of a couple affected by lack of self-control? Lack of self-control in eating leads to gluttony, which leads to illness. No control over time results in lack of achievement and living in mediocrity, which leads to inferiority. Lack of energy management leads to the depletion of the dynamic force that moves every man. Lack of discretion in purchasing depletes man's financial resources. When we meditate on thought control, the grace of God within helps us to treat ourselves well from even the most terrifying illnesses. Meditation is an excellent cleaning method of our minds and souls. In meditation, we are cleaning our mind from the lack of self-control. Emotions follow thoughts. Thought control is followed by cleaning our souls from disturbing emotions. Let us ask ourselves how many times we have cleaned our driveway, garage, houses, cars, desks, bathrooms, porches, and kitchens, but we did not clean even for one time our minds or our souls. The yearning for true joy brings us to the need for urgent medication to clear our minds and souls through meditation.

Our feelings, health, talk, actions, and reactions are the direct results of our thoughts. Controlling our thoughts by meditation will bring all of these to the ultimate perfection. Man is not what he thinks of himself; he is the sum of his thoughts. Man may daydream that he is great, but in reality, he is not even willing to wake from his dream to make himself great. However, if a man always thinks loving and kind thoughts, he will be a loving and kind person. Everything we do in our life is based on and determined by the quality of our thinking. When we have high quality thoughts, we will have high quality actions. When we have high quality of thoughts, we will have a high quality of life. When we have positive thoughts, we can make the best of our present and will have a good future. When we have healthy thoughts, we will have healthy bodies and spirits. High quality thoughts are pure and good thoughts. These thoughts are the antidote for depression, anxiety, pity, sorrow, disappointment, or incompetence. When we govern our thoughts by meditation, we can think clearly. When we can think clearly, we can realize our weaknesses and overcome them. Only then will we allow pure and gentle thoughts to flourish. Hence after, our lives become magnificent.

Pondering the power of thoughts and their effects on man's life is astonishing. A thought is the seed of an action. However, if an action is done on the level of thought, it is mental action. That mental action is equivalent to a physical action for which we will give an account on the day of judgment. The Lord Jesus Christ teaches us that if a man looks and lusts, he has already committed that action (Matthew 5:28). Then Paul the Apostle reminds us saying, "... in the day when God will judge the secrets of men by Jesus Christ, according to my gospel" (Romans 2:16). Considering these two verses places *a thought is an action* at a higher level. Pondering these two fundamental biblical verses reveals to us our deep need to use our thoughts in the right way. We need to bless and heal by our thoughts. If we take the verse of Matthew 5:28 and phrase it another way, it will be as follows: If a man looks at a man and blesses him, he already blessed him. Or if a man looks at an ill person and asks the Father for healing, he presents him for Divine healing. These are blessing and healing actions done on the mental level. Meditation makes us use our thoughts with the right applications such as these - healing and blessing. Meditation of thought control empowers us to direct our thoughts to positive mental action that soon will give rise to physical action. It is remarkable that we will give an account of both the mental actions as well as the physical ones.

Meditation teaches us the magnificent changing of our mental attitude toward life, from negative to positive, from depression to joy, from dying to healing, from failure to success, from impossible to possible, from revenge to forgiveness, and from weakness to strength. It has great impact on changing our train of thoughts. Man's mental attitude toward circumstances, not the circumstances, determines his happiness or misery. Man's positive attitude redirects negative circumstances to positive outcomes. We can change our circumstances by changing our mental attitude. In other words, when we change our mental attitude towards circumstances, the outcomes of these circumstances will change. If the reality is bad, what is our reaction toward it? Is it positive or negative? With a positive mental attitude, we always find the alternative possible solutions for difficulties that seem to be impossible. The way we react reveals who we are. We are sons of God. Christ lives in us and loves us. God gave us the spirit of power, and it is odd for us to have a negative mental attitude and a weak spirit. "God has not given us a spirit of fear, but of power and of love and of a sound mind" (2 Timothy 1:7).

(2) Focusing

Man's focus is the sunshine that brings attention to different life aspects in a well-rounded manner. When man's thoughts are controlled, man can focus on what he needs to achieve. When man governs his thoughts and senses, he can focus on the goals and the purpose of his life. Since there are numerous aspects of our lives, it can be a challenge to know *on what and when to focus*. It can be tough to focus on health, spirituality, education, career, job, marriage, raising children, and the house. Then there is a great need to focus on the One who will direct us to what we ought to focus on in each phase of our lives. We need to focus on Christ, and He will guide our mental focusing powers. Only when man focuses on Christ does his mind become very powerful and alert. The mere focusing on Christ is the core for success in man's life.

Thought control that is expressed in time management and energy expenditure discretion brings us to the realization that continuous use of technology decreases our mental focus function. On the contrary, decisiveness of correctly using technology can boost our focus to an optimal level. Using technology in education, communication, or work are just simple examples for its correct use. However, with using technology there many distractions because of notification, constant dependency, connectedness, or negativity of information. This is when meditation is needed for decisiveness to regenerate mental focusing.

Meditation and mental focusing function as a cause and effect relationship. Meditation harnesses the mental focusing. Mental focusing results in effective mediation. Mediation creates a mental firewall against distraction, and it empowers us to be focused. In a practical way of focusing mental power, man needs to write his thoughts and know what to focus on. Writing one's thoughts is the way that man can see his thoughts. Hence after, he can determine what is positive and what is negative. He then can pursue the positive ones to foster and translate them into plans and actions. He needs to review this list frequently to see what he achieved yesterday, what he can achieve today, and what will be achieved tomorrow. The direct jewel results of mental focusing are the ability to allocate time and energy to the must-do list or things you need to achieve, as well as how to use your time efficiently.

There are helpful tools and techniques for focusing. *In Christ, I control my Thoughts and my Senses; I Am Focused* is the primary mental tool for focusing. In addition, a tangible art craft with inspiring quotes or biblical verses can be helpful tools to focus. Specifying a certain day during the week to build the habit for focusing as well as choosing a quiet area in the house can be another helpful tool. Although these tools and techniques may vary from one to another, one can start with the common tools until he develops his own with the goal to master focusing.

Keep your face to the sunshine and you cannot see a shadow.[9] We see shadows in life because we do not focus on the sun that is Christ. These shadows are failures and uncertainty. No one has known Christ and not succeeded or achieved. Christ can be realized through silence, thought control, and taming of the senses. Reciting the name of the Lord Jesus Christ gives us a mental firewall against the darts of the devil that tend to distract us. Reciting the affirmation In *Christ, I control my Thoughts and my Senses; I Am Focused* girds our mental power for a high level of focusing. This affirmation implies that *I Am Focused* to complete the work that Heavenly Father gave me to do. This affirmation releases the power of the mind to serenity for deep thinking. The more we are focused, the more we are able to use the full capacity of our minds. The more we are focused, the more we are able to function in spite of the turmoil of this world. The more we focus on Christ, the more He reveals to us the purpose of our lives. Only those who master focusing their mental powers are able to fully accomplish what Christ designed as purpose for their lives.

12: In Christ, I Am Patience, Perseverance, Positivity, and Persistence. I Am Accuracy and Understanding.

(1) Patience

The secret behind mastering any skill and any great achievement is mastering patience, perseverance, positivity, and persistence, as well as accuracy and understanding. Start with patience and the rest will follow. Life is full of ongoing challenges, and no one is free from these challenges. A great component of these challenges is dealing with the continual life changes in everything around us. Other challenges can be financial, marital, jobs and career ups and downs, and daily dealings with some people who are not applying God's principles of love and kindness. Patience is a vital pillar in sustaining a steady life, and it can save lives.

A business man was facing a financial hardship. He decided that taking his own life was the solution for this difficulty. Well, of course it was not Christ who was telling this man to do so. It was the Adversary. With Christ, there is no despair or impossibility. He travelled to another city, where he once conducted part of his business activity. Walking in the streets to take in his last scenes of the world before he put an end to his life, the man passed by a street merchant saying "patience" frequently. That business man stood across from that merchant and felt this was a message from God to him. So he returned to his room in the hotel and wrote *patience* on a piece of paper. He kept meditating on that simple word. He kept repeating it as frequently as that street merchant was saying it. The grace of God was bestowed on this man and he did not take his life.

The following morning, he received a call from his assistant stating that one of the banks agreed to help the firm and work a financial plan to overcome the current hardship. It is amazing that just meditating on the simple word *patience* had saved that man's life.

If God is patient with us while we are rejecting Him, and still sends His sun and mercies on earth every day, we ought to have patience with each other. His patience with us is for our salvation and repentance. Patience provides us with the mental attitude of endurance, which in turn will help us to walk through life's challenges and hardships. We need to be patient and never give up until we overcome our weakness, until spouses change behaviors for the sake of love, until the children do things in the right way, until the teenager becomes wise and understands life, until finding the right job, and until the promotion comes as recognition for our hard work. We need to be patient with ourselves until we reach the level of spiritual awareness that is developed through meditation. We need to meditate on patience until it becomes our second nature and until we reap its rewards.

The challenge with patience, as with many other good traits, is that most of us think we have patience until we come across adversity that tests our patience. And then we find we don't have patience. One matter that tests our patience, for instance, is last-minute help needed at work. Most of us start to think about going home and relaxing. Usually this happens toward the end of work activity and at the end of the work day. Then all of a sudden, someone shows up who needs our help. This situation brings frustration to those who have no patience. After many years experiencing such unexpected events, I've learned the following techniques are great assets to boost one's patience. First: expect that last-minute help requests could happen. This help could be needed by a co-worker, or something urgent may need to be fixed or modified, requiring one to stay longer hours. It can be a customer showing up at the last minute before closing. Knowing that these things can happen can relieve the surprise factor. Second: we need to take these situations in a positive way and exercise our inner strength; exercise our patience and kindness. Third: refrain from stating what the situation would be if the last-minute need hadn't shown up. It is common to hear such statements as, "I could be home", or "I could be enjoying my dinner." Doing so does not help boost one's patience.

In a big hospital where every minute counts for every employee as well as the patients, a pharmacy employee received a call seeking help with a technical issue. This call was the second one as the caller had contacted him previously and was referred to another department specializing in this kind of issue. The employee was busy at the end of his shift, nevertheless he decided to help the caller. The supervisor was overhearing the conversation. After the employee resolved the caller's issue and finished with the call, the supervisor told him, "You have the patience of the saints."

In Christ, I Am Patience is the medication for a short temper. As we are children of God, we are a reflection of His patience. God is the Whole patience and we are channels of the Divine patience on earth. The affirmation *I Am Patience* expands our tolerance for the faults of others. It is the remedy for bearing or dealing with people who have a short temper. When we master patience, we influence others positively to a higher level of awareness of their attitude without hurting their feelings for their lack of the virtue of patience. Adding strength to another strength will make great power. Adding patience to silence will bring forth powerful character. With that character man can positively affect his environment with tremendous influence, as well as face the least amount of opposition from it. Through patience and silence, we realize that no one is perfect nor is anyone without burden.

Through applying these magnificent spiritual principles, we support each other as Christ want us to do. Only then do we perfect our calling that we are children of the Heavenly Father, who sustains all His creation.

(2) Perseverance

If we only work when we feel good, we will get nothing done. So there is a need for prevailing merit that empowers us to work while we are tired, not feeling well, running low on energy, or did not get enough sleep. This merit is perseverance. The bright future is the offspring of a beautiful dream in the present that we pursued and achieved. A bright future does not happen accidently. It requires some quality factors such as hard work, determination, and perseverance. A beautiful dream creates an inner mental image, which in turn will make us to align our path and gird ourselves with these qualities. Achievers are those who are able to translate their dreams into organized thoughts, and then put these thoughts into actions. Achievers are the ones who persevered regardless the reality of current circumstances. Successful people don't wait for circumstances to become better so they can start school or to change to a career they'd always hoped for. "He who observes the wind will not sow, and he who regards the clouds will not reap" (Ecclesiastes 11:4). As long as there is a green light from the Almighty, persevere and start to change what is needed to change. As a result, the circumstances will be better. We then will find ourselves in a cycle of perseverance and effort leading to good results and good results lead to increased perseverance and effort. Those who achieved what seemed impossible started by doing little things. *Start by doing what's necessary; then do what's possible; and suddenly you are doing the impossible.*[10]

In Christ, I Am Perseverance is the treatment for overcoming unwanted reality while praying and hoping for a better reality.

Most of us are challenged by undesirable circumstances, and we need to pray for these circumstances to change. However, negative emotions form resistance to praying. The result is losing hope, and circumstances stay as they are. Perseverance is the right tool that equips us to proceed with prayers and hope for change.

A wife was angry with her husband because of disagreement about a certain matter. The wife wanted to spend her free time in serving the Lord and helping out in charitable deeds. Despite the fact that she took care of her house and nothing was out of order, the husband was upset. After hearing the story from both sides, the recommendation to the wife was to pray that God resolve this disagreement. "How can I pray for him when I am angry at him?" she asked. Will being angry resolve this disagreement? Of course not! However, her perseverance in prayer and overcoming negative emotions was the right maneuver in resolving the matter. She persevered and things became better. After a few months, the husband started to help his wife in her service.

"Blessed is the man who endures temptation; for when he has been approved, he will receive the crown of life which the Lord has promised to those who love Him" (James 1:12). Perseverance is the means for enduring life's temptations. The rewards are double. On earth problems get solved and in heaven we receive the crown of life. Meditation on perseverance is the path of overcoming giving up and despair. To win and overcome hardship is to never quit. The affirmation *In Christ, I Am Perseverance* builds a mental setting that one will not accept unwanted reality and life adversity, and will change it through prayer and through the help of Christ.

(3) Positivity

We live in a world full of negativity. Most of us who recognize this trait wish there was an empty corner in the universe free from negativity to live in. The dynamic force behind the world's negativity is the devil. "We know that we are of God, and the whole world lies under the sway of the wicked one" (1 John 5:19). Through this negativity, he influences peoples' lives. Through this influence, whirlpools of actions and reactions that are against God's commandments dominate the world. A man divorces his wife after many years of marriage and love. A youth dishonors his parents who want him to be wise and successful. The value of friendship has diminished and materialism controls peoples' lives. Life became about who gets the most advanced technology, the biggest house, and the luxury cars. Yet while having the most comfortable life, the least opposition disturbs our minds with the result being weak and unpeaceable minds. Odds and conflicts fill our lives. Some indulge with food, but want to be slim and healthy. Some wish for a luxurious life but only through winning the lottery, not through hard work. As a result of these negatives, we seek human counselors for sets of rules that are man-made. We forget to counsel with God and pray, and we set His simple Ten Commandments aside. Others can't face and cope with life and go to doctors for pills to ease their minds.

A positive attitude is the solution for the world's negativity. Positivity comes by claiming our sonship to the Sole Source of an upright attitude, God. It is then we can overcome the world. "For whatever is born of God overcomes the world. "And this is the victory that has overcome the world - our faith" (1 John 5:4). The greatest unique, positive character, who overcame the world is Christ. The woman caught in the very act of adultery, He didn't judge. The woman who'd had five husbands, He preached to her and gave her the living water. When Thomas doubted His resurrection, He assured and blessed those who believe yet have not seen. Peter denied Him, yet He loved and assigned him to take care of His sheep. The woman sick for twelve years, He healed. Paul persecuted the church, but Christ appeared to him and made him a preacher.

In Christ Meditation is the fundamental and most needed affirmation to restore the positive attitude into our lives. As light chases darkness, our positivity gets rid of negativity. Meditation on positivity empowers us to live as children of God and in Christ-like character. It is only then we heed His deeds and act like Christ. "For I have given you an example, that you should do as I have done to you" (John 13:15). When we react to peoples' negative actions with a positive attitude, we will always be in peace and in power. When we focus on the positive aspect of a matter, we will always be able to react positively. Only when we adopt the positive attitude mentality, do our lives change for the better. A positive attitude mentality seeks to solve problems and not to escape problems. Positive mentality believes that nothing is impossible for Christ to resolve, for with Him all things are possible. Only then will we have harmonious happy marriages, children honoring their parents, successful lives, and peace that surpasses man's mind.

(4) Persistence

Success and achievements are attained by continuous collaborative work. This requires persistence and patience. Persistence is doing whatever is necessary for success over and over regardless the opposition or unsuccessful attempts, until one reaches his goal. Success in the spiritual life necessitates persistence in reading the Bible, applying its principles, and praying on a regular basis. While this is true, praying for life subjects requires persistence in faith. Lack of persistence in faith falls into irregular prayer, which in turn leads to not attaining what is prayed for. "But let him ask in faith, with no doubting, for he who doubts is like a wave of the sea driven and tossed by the wind. For let not that man suppose that he will receive anything from the Lord" (James 1:6-7). Persistence is from the Lord; lack of persistence is temptation from the devil. Many of us did not receive our requests from the Lord, and were eventually convinced by the devil to stop praying. The devil succeeded in entrapping some of us with the thought, "maybe God is not willing to give you this request." However, through persistence the blind man got healed. "He cried out all the more, 'Son of David, have mercy on me!'" (Mark 10:48). He received his sight because he was persistent in his request and did not let the Lord go without healing him. When we are challenged by lack of persistence in prayer and by doubts, we need to remember that He instructed us to ask that we would receive. Also, when we are living righteously, He will not hold back what is good from us. "No good thing will He withhold from those who walk uprightly" (Psalm 84:11).

In Christ, I Am Persistence is the affirmation that feeds our zeal to keep going until goals are attained. Persistence in meditation results in perfection of meditation and increased attention and focus. Persistence in repentance makes man rise again even after falling seven times (Proverbs 24:16). Persistence in forgiveness releases man's mind from hatred, and to receive forgiveness himself from the Lord. Persistence in forgiveness can be up to seventy times seven (Matthew 18:22). Persistence in prayer builds strong bonds to our Lord, establishes peace of mind, and prayers get answered (Luke 18:7). The mere persistence of thanksgiving and praising God in prayer is a clear sign of loving the Lord. Persistence in nourishing love to our spouses results in happy marriages. Persistence in finding out our children's talents and nurturing them leads to well-rounded and successful children.

In Christ, I Am Patience, Perseverance, Positivity, and Persistence.

I Am Accuracy and Understanding.

Our success is the direct result of being persistent in doing whatever is legitimate to succeed and proceed in life.

(5) Accuracy

God has the absolute accuracy and we have relative accuracy. Discerning this concept makes us realize the immeasurable accuracy of God. With this accuracy, He holds the earth in its orbit the exact distance from the sun to provide day and night. He established heavens and set boundaries to the oceans, seas, and the rivers. With the same accuracy, He prepared for every one of us the satisfying career, the peaceful home, the dependable car, the faithful spouse, and the beautiful children even before we show up in our journey on earth. It is this accuracy that numbered our hairs. "But the very hairs of your head are all numbered" (Luke 12:7). The accuracy of His mercy counted the rewards for a cup of water (Matthew 10:42) and the coins of the poor widow (Luke 21: 3). All we have to do is to believe and trust in His accuracy and timing.

Meditation on accuracy motivates us to live in Christ's accuracy. *I Am Accuracy* is the reflection of Christ's accuracy. *In Christ, I Am Accuracy* is the affirmation that makes us assess every thought, every word, and every action. When meditation on accuracy is refined, the more we are perfected in our ways of thinking, talking, and processing life. We need accuracy in using our time and energy. We need accuracy in our jobs. We need accuracy in every aspect of our lives. Meditation on accuracy is the key that unlocks the power of precision. Only when this power is released, will one be accurate in processing only positive thoughts and rejecting negative ones. With accuracy, the needed amount of food will be purchased. With that accuracy, man will consume what is needed, and there will be no excess that causes extra weight. With accuracy, man will buy what is needed and no junk will be accumulated in the house or the closets. With accuracy, man will be precise in his words. With accuracy, we will distinguish what deeds will present Christ and what deeds are deception from the enemy. *In Christ, I Am Accuracy* is the motive that enables us to provide accurate deeds as children of God. It is then these deeds will shine to the world and people will glorify our Heavenly Father.

(6) Understanding

Understanding is the basis for using man's mental faculties. These faculties are among God's supreme gifts to the human race. Using these faculties is one of the necessities in our lives. Understanding is one of the beautiful jewels of a sound mind. As we are sons and daughters of God and the Spirit of God dwells in us, we are blessed to have sound minds. "For God has not given us a spirit of fear, but of power and of love and of a sound mind" (2 Timothy 1:7). A man filled with and guided by God's Spirit will always develop a sound mind and have understanding.

There is an ongoing and very interesting challenge in our world: many people have understanding of worldly matters but not of spiritual matters. We see on a daily basis brothers and sisters around us, who understand many aspects of life. However, when it comes to spiritual matters, they have no care for such. They may understand economy, stocks, career developments, finance and savings, cars, health, politics, sports, traveling and best places for vacations, real estate, investments, and many other earthly aspects. But when it comes to their salvation and eternity, they may have no clue. About those people the Bible says, "He has blinded their eyes and hardened their hearts, lest they should see with their eyes, lest they should understand with their hearts and turn, so that I should heal them" (John 12:40). The devil has played his tactics very well with such people. He caused them to use their minds' faculties in earthly matters only, but not the spiritual ones.

A man filled with God's Spirit will understand earthly as well as spiritual matters. This understanding will empower him to process life with wisdom, knowing that we are all on a journey and will one day leave this temporal world and transition into eternity. This understanding will make man balance his life wisely among all its aspects and activities.

In the natural and simple view, how can a man understand every phase of his life? How can a man pass successfully from one phase to another? How can a man understand himself? How can he understand the meaning and the purpose of his life? How can a man understand everything about marriage and how to have a successful marriage? How can a man secure his marriage against all the never-ending challenges? How can a man know and understand how to raise his children in a godly manner despite all the traps in the world? How can he understand and deal with people who may not have the same morals, and still bring the light of Christ into his work place? How can a man understand that on the day of God's judgment, he will give an account for all of his thoughts, words and deeds?

The answer for all these challenging questions is very simple. It is the understanding of life through Christ. The affirmation *In Christ, I Am Understanding* means I understand how to process my life through Christ. In a deeper insight, it means I am making myself sensitive to the Spirit of God, Who will help me to do the right thing at the right time. *In Christ, I Am Understanding* makes the meditator seek to understand the spiritual matters as well as the earthly matters. Meditation on understanding makes the meditator understand those earthly matters and process them discreetly without losing sight of heavenly goals. It is only through trusting and accepting Christ's guidance, that a man will know how to choose his right career, how to choose the right spouse, when to start a family, and how to raise children. Still, while handling all these matters of life, a man keeps track of his spirituality and his eyes focused on eternity.

In a sequential manner, every affirmation leads to another; each affirmation becomes both the cause and the effect of the next one. A man with a pure mind will always feel God and will feel good. "Blessed are the pure in heart, for they shall see God" (Matthew 5:8). A man who feels God will love Him. A man who loves God and feels God's love will trust God and will have no fear. Trusting God is the result of strong faith and vice versa. A humble man will have thanksgiving and obedience. The Lord blesses a humble, obedient man with wisdom and discernment. Silence is the fruit of great wisdom. As a matter of fact, silence is wisdom. A wise man can always control his thoughts and his senses. Then through wisdom and silence, that man can listen and understand. A man of understanding and focused on Christ, will always know what to do and when to do it. A man with patience and perseverance will know how to proceed in life despite all opposition. The beauty of these affirmations is that they are the results of one's vivid meditation and real-life experience. These affirmations are connected to each other and every one can be a starting point for magnificent change in one's life. While this is true, all of them lead to one goal, which is to live our lives as Christ-like persons.

13: In Christ, I Am Optimism. I have Hope and Willpower.

(1) Optimism

Optimism is the ability to make one's mind work in his favor. It is the mental attitude to see the sun shining behind the dark clouds. It is the tendency to be confident about a good future. Optimism is the expectancy for the best outcome. It is the trust that makes a man believe that all things work together for good to those who love the Lord (Romans 8:28). Optimism is especially required in facing challenges. Since life is full of challenges, optimism is always needed.

If optimism is making one's mind to revolve clockwise, and pessimism is revolving counter-clock wise, why would one not determine to make his mind go in the direction of optimism? Anticipation determines outcomes. Positive anticipation attracts positive outcomes. If we desire good outcomes, we must in faith expect these outcomes and patiently anticipate to receive them from the Divine Providence. This expectancy happens through optimism and faith. If faith is the conception of good results from within, optimism is the anticipation of these good results until they become our reality. Faith has two brothers - hope and optimism. They go hand in hand. A man with faith will always have hope and be optimistic; an optimistic man will always have faith and hope.

Considering that the main components of man's life are time and energy, pessimism is a waste of time and energy. In a given span of time, if one spent that time in pessimistic thoughts of outcomes, which he actually does not want to happen, he wasted that time and his mental energy. On the other hand, if he spent the same given time in optimistic thoughts, he would receive what he needs by expectancy, and that time and energy would be well used. The question is, why do some of us tend to think pessimistic thoughts and not optimistic ones? The devil has succeeded in making those who think pessimistically believe they are being realistic. Being realistic is to consciously know and understand the present circumstance. Being pessimistic is having a negative attitude toward a circumstance, which can make one feel helpless and hopeless. Being optimistic is having a desire to change an existing condition for a better one in the future; one that will have a positive outcome. Optimism is a gracious gift from God that inspires us to ask according to His will.

As everything in life needs training, being optimistic needs practice and techniques too. First: find the positive side in any matter. If things seem disturbing, one needs to ask himself, *What is the positive side of this situation?*

A classmate was in a car accident that was not her fault. The report stated "no fault" and the car was designated "totaled" by the insurance company. Despite the fact that she had some financial tightness, she found the positive side of driving a new car and being thankful she had no back injury. That classmate showed one level of optimism and thanksgiving. It is our choice and conscious decision to find the bright side of any circumstance. Second: intend to make the best of every day of your life. It seems that many stereotype the entire day from an incident that happened at the beginning of the day, even a common occurrence such as a flat tire, heavy rain, cloudy weather, a call about an unpaid insurance claim, or even spilled coffee on a dress or shirt. Then people keep talking about these things the rest of the day, some even for several days. Consider silencing your mind and tongue when tempted to repeat or talk about such events. If an unpleasant incident happens during the day, it does not mean the whole day will be like that. Optimistic people have their climate inside and nothing from outside will change that inner climate. Third: stay away from those who speak in a pessimistic manner and in doubt. Pessimism can be contagious for those who try to be optimistic when optimism is not yet ingrained and established in their mind.

In Christ, I Am Optimism is the empowering assertion to help us to be optimistic. The affirmations of the *In Christ Meditation* are well-arranged in a purposeful, sequential manner. Prior to the affirmation of optimism, there is an affirmation of thought-control. Controlling one's thoughts is the determining factor for one steering his thoughts clockwise or counter-clockwise, optimistically or pessimistically. And then the affirmation *In Christ, I Am Optimism* is the dynamic factor for being optimistic. It may take time for some of us to leave pessimism and go in the optimistic direction. However, practicing meditation is the beneficial technique for this path. In addition, proclaiming this positive manner of thinking in the name of Christ is the seal that will ingrain it, no matter what opposition one may face. When optimism becomes our habitual thinking, we will develop a sound mind and healthy body, and will receive what we hoped for. When we are empowered by optimism, we see success attainable in every aspect of life.

(2) Hope

Again, hope is the sibling of optimism. Both make one expect goodness. It is the inner yearning that all things will work for good regardless what the reality seems. Hope is the inner conviction that arouses us to work toward our desired goals. Man, with hope for a good life, will have a good life no matter how long the way. A man who has lost hope has lost all things. We need to have hope that we will succeed in our careers, that we will find the right jobs, that we will find the right spouse, that we will see goodness in our children, and that we will fulfill the purpose of our life. Losing hope is from the enemy. Hope is from the Lord of Hope, Jesus Christ.

A retired veteran hopes to get a job in the healthcare administration field. As he was telling me his story, I perceived he is just moving from one phase to another phase in his life and every phase is filled with hope. He joined the Army in his twenties, then founded a happy family. After he retired, he pursued his old dream to be a healthcare administrator, and he has never given up. At the end of our inspiring chat, he told me this, "If God does not lose hope in me, why should I lose hope in myself?"

To develop hope, intentionally repeat very often the affirmation of *In Christ, I Am Optimism; I have Hope and Willpower.* This will lift up our mood and focus our minds on Christ, hence our spirits will be receptive to the guidance of the Holy Spirit. The more we sincerely repeat this statement, the more our thought rise above any disturbing and negative issues of life. The more this affirmation is ingrained in our minds, the more we focus on the desired goals and what we hope to achieve, and the less we focus on obstacles. The challenge is that some of us focus on obstacles, which in turn magnify them to be bigger than our hope. Our perception of life's circumstances will change when we change ourselves. Trying to change our lives without correcting ourselves is like treating symptoms and not the illness itself.

Meditation on hope will inspire us to see our hope is as big as the blue sky. Through that hope we visualize the unseen blessings until they become reality. Through that hope we focus our imagination to expect good things. Through that hope we persevere in prayer and meditation until the good outcomes show up. When we fill ourselves with hope through spiritual meditation and biblical affirmation, hope will fill all aspects of our lives.

(3) Willpower

Willpower is the firmness to carry on until one reaches what he has hoped for. It is the unseen intellectual strength to plan and act to reach dreams. Our willpower is naturally strong because we originated from God, who is the Sole Source of all might. Allowing negative thoughts from the devil to creep into our minds will weaken our minds, and in turn weaken our willpower. At this point in this meditation series, we need to ponder things in one way or the other. We need to ponder whether a thought is from God or from the devil. Meditation awakens us to recognize the nature of a thought. Not only this, but also it is the fire-wall that keeps our minds in a protected state so thoughts from the devil do not penetrate our minds. It is vital to remember that a thought is not of oneself until one meditates on it. Both the beauty and the risk of this is that sooner or later one will act upon the ongoing thought. Once a man starts to act on a thought, that thought becomes his and will manifest in reality. It is the relentless work of the devil to send all kinds of thoughts to human beings to weaken their willpower. Once man loses his willpower, he becomes prey in the hands of the devil. This is why some of us eat unhealthy food despite many alarming health conditions. Others still drive fast regardless the number of tickets and the driving points needing to be resolved. Others are entrapped in addiction, cyber sensuality, adultery, addiction, and alcoholism. The devil stole their willpower and now rules them as puppets in his hands.

In addition to targeting our time and energy, the devil targets our will. He uses the concept that we have free will to do whatever we want; that we can try new things and then repent. Once we do something against God, we lose our free will and feel disconnected from God. Hence after, our free will is in the grip of the devil. Now if man's will is a gift from God and the devil always wants to steal it, it is man's prudence to keep his will with God so the devil does not steal it. Who is mightier than God that can steal man's will from Him? No one! However, it is man's free will to give his will back to God. This is a simple fact. If we have something precious, we need to keep it with whoever can protect it. I know a father who gave his child a watch. A few days later, the child refrained from taking the watch to school and returned it to his dad for safe-keeping, telling him that he will use it when he is around. It is ironic that this child realized that if he would like to keep something precious, he should keep it with his dad. Some of us did not realize this simple concept, and the devil easily stole our will from us.

There is a hope and treatment for every matter. With God all things are possible. The ultimate goal of man is to regain his will and live in accordance to God's commandments. Once a man obeys God and follows His commandments, Christ will restore his will. Regained will is the result of obedience to Christ. *In Christ Meditation* is the magnificent medication for weak and stolen willpower. To restore and strengthen our willpower, we need to ponder effective remedies. First: recite frequently the affirmation – *In Christ, I Am Optimism; I have Hope and Willpower.* Reciting the name of Christ rejects that devil who is fighting our willpower. When reciting is perfected in practice, all mental powers will gradually be focused, and you will see hope to regain your willpower. You will observe the amount of calories you take in. Health and ideal weight will be regained. You will see change in your pattern of thinking. Confident self-dignity and positive self-image will be regained. The affirmation – *In Christ, I Am Optimism, I have Hope and Willpower* is Divinely inspired to treat various intellectual afflictions. The mere act of repeating this affirmation is the beginning of regaining your willpower. Second: when the Lord motivates us to do something and we sense any opposition of inability, we need to recite this, "I can do all things through Christ who strengthens me" (Philippians 4:13). Repeating this positive statement and parallel biblical verses generates a state of authorization and acknowledgment in the inner being, which in turn brings the mind into a "can do" attitude. Remember positive affirmation empowers man over circumstances. Third: practice strengthens your willpower by starting with something little such as, "I won't drink soda for two days." This will make your mind determine that you have willpower over drinking soda. Once you prove to yourself that you can do something little, you will move on to another thing that can be bigger, and so on. Day by day, you will gain strong willpower, and you will realize that you can do everything that your mind determines through the help of the Lord. Once willpower is gained, we need to continue the meditation and prayer that Christ guards and guides our willpower.

14: In Christ, I Am Calmness and Confidence. I Am Gentleness.

(1) Calmness

Calmness is the fruit of wisdom. Calmness of mind is strength. "In quietness and confidence shall be your strength" (Isaiah 30:15). Calmness is the result of trusting God. A man who trusts God will have stillness in the middle of a storm. "Trust in the Lord with all your heart, and lean not on your own understanding" (Proverbs 3:5). We have the tendency to be calm because we, through Christ, are children of God and the Holy Spirit lives within us. The Holy Spirit guides us to what we need to do and how we react in different encounters. God is the Whole calmness and we, His children, part of His calmness. Calmness is the result of believing that God is managing every second and every step of our lives. No matter what we face, He is there (Psalm 23:4). Through calmness we perceive His presence and can listen to His guidance.

Calmness is the peaceable state of mind. It is the tranquility of one's inner being. It has nothing to do with where we live or work. Calmness is greatly fed on the sacred spiritual rapport of man and God. When our father Adam lost that peace with God, he lost his calmness and feared. He lost his calmness despite the fact he was still in the Garden of Eden. This explains why many of us in these days have the highest technology and live in luxurious houses yet do not have calmness. Moreover, some go to doctors to appease their anxiety and fear by taking pills that give them temporary calmness. God is inside every man. When we reconcile with ourselves, we are reconciling with God, who is within. When we reconcile with God, we will have calmness. Calmness is the result of walking in God's ways, and He will restore our peace despite the devil's opposition and adversity. "When a man's ways please the Lord, He makes even his enemies to be at peace with him" (Proverbs 16:7).

Our calmness is tested when the devil sends someone our way to annoy us. We need to remember that the devil does not appear to us to say, "I am the enemy of the human race and I want to annoy and bother you." However, the enemy will send people who yielded their will to be tools in his hands to bother his brother or sister. If we remember this fact, we will react with calmness. As a matter of fact, our calmness will annoy the devil, but it may awake the person used by him to pursue calmness. Any man who tries to bother another is driven by the human Adversary to do so.

A supervisor sent an email to the employees in his department with instructions, dates, and times about an upcoming event. This email contained a mistake. One employee sent a private email to that manager to notate the mistake and avoid potential unwanted consequences. Instead of being thankful and appreciative, the supervisor got offended and began to trouble that employee by asking about unfinished projects put on hold by the leadership, and about a fraction of overtime worked involuntarily by the employee. As this employee was calm and responded wisely, the supervisor got annoyed by the calmness and commented on his stillness and tranquility. That employee won a great battle with just the simple inner strength of calmness.

Thinking and feeling are ongoing internal processes within every human being. Man's feelings have tremendous effects on the way he handles and processes his life. If one wants to process his life in a positive way, he must be conscious of his feelings. Challenges arise because the majority of us are not conscious of the effects of our feelings on processing our lives, as well as our inability to deal with negative emotions arising from our daily routines. Man strives to foster pleasant feelings and subdue unpleasant ones. Another challenge arises when man does not realize certain feelings. This in turn makes them harder to deal with. In a simple way, man needs to be conscious of his feelings and acknowledge them so he can deal with them. Meditation helps man to be conscious of his feelings. The underlying principle of this magnificent result is that meditation fosters calmness in man's mind, allowing him to give attention to his feelings. Meditation inspires us to be spirit- and mind-driven, and not feelings-driven. A lot of the problems we experience arise from being feelings-driven. To make the subject more complex, the majority of these feelings are negative and their presence unidentified. Meditation on calmness can be the remedy for negative feelings.

Some of us were born with the nature of being calm. Others did not have this inheritance. For those who run short in their heritage of calmness, there is a remedy, which is meditation. Meditation on calmness ingrains this beautiful jewel until it becomes our nature. When we recognize the living of Christ within, we will be calm. Christ is calm all the time, and as we find this treasure through sacred rapport, we can be calm all the time. We then will manifest calmness in all aspects of our lives. Calmness starts from within and is then expressed to the outer surroundings. We will be calm in our speech, actions, and reactions. When we are calm in our speech, the tone of our voice will be soft and our words will be "seasoned with salt", imparting grace to the hearer (Colossians 4:6). When we are calm, we will not be offended by persons or circumstances. On the contrary, continuous tranquility will be our natural state. Calmness and thought control are cause and effect. A man who is able to control his thoughts will be calm. A calm person will always control his thoughts. *In Christ, I Am Calmness* is the driving affirmation that inspires us to be calm. It is then we can positively influence our own lives and the world around us as Christ wants us to.

(2) Confidence

The secret of being confident is reliance on God. Reliance on God results from our knowing He lives inside us. Consciousness that Christ lives in us and loves us is the result of calmness, and calmness is the result of meditation on Christ. Hence after, our confidence will be evident. To have confidence, we only need to recognize Christ is within. Merely recognizing the living of Christ within us is the beginning of confidence. Then we will be confident that everything will work for good no matter what we encounter. We will be confident that God is managing all aspects of our lives for the best. We will be confident that our lives are orchestrated even to the minor details by His Divine power. Confidence and assurance are a reflection of trusting God. The confident man emits positive thoughts and attitudes all around him, which in turn lead to positive outcomes. Confidence is the reflection of faith, which puts man in harmony with himself and his surroundings. On the contrary, fear and discord are the result of disbelief and doubt. These are from the enemy. Confidence and assurance are from God.

Confidence is one of the important pillars of success. Success is the result of a positive attitude for processing life. Confidence is built by practice and training. Man needs to train himself to trust in God's given abilities to proceed and succeed in life. Failure is the result of fear and lack of confidence. By these, man attracts to himself what he does not want. "For the thing I greatly feared has come upon me, and what I dreaded has happened to me" (Job 3:25). In a simple way, we need to be careful not think on what we do not want to manifest in our lives. Thinking on something that we don't want will cause it to manifest, regardless the fact that it is what we want to avoid. When in doubt and lack of confidence, man needs to face himself before the consequences of these traits come upon him. We need to practice confidence to achieve a steady state that sustains our success and endeavors in life. This practice will come by meditation on confidence and speaking faith and positive words to ourselves.

A twelve-year-old boy chanted a song in the church choir at one of the events. He sang his part very well and received great compliments afterwards. That child has no more talent than his friends; however, his parents were diligent to encourage him and make him practice over and over. This practice boosted his level of confidence, which in turn helped him to chant very well.

In general, people tend to listen and pay attention to those who speak and act with great confidence. They infer that this person likes and masters what he is doing, and this attraction is a tendency in human behavior. It is an excellent idea to practice and boost our confidence before certain activities such as public speaking, sport games, business presentations, or singing in a choir.

There are a few hindrances for man to be confident and not to lose confidence in himself. These can be mistakes of the past or unwise decisions that still affect the present. The remedy for this lack of confidence is to understand that no one will learn and have experience in life without making some mistakes. Those who do not make mistakes do not accomplish anything in their lives, and actually they do not exist. On the contrary, a wise man can learn from his mistakes and the mistakes of others to avoid them, lest one day these mistakes will become his. A wise man learns the art of turning his mistakes and weaknesses into cornerstones of strength and bright change in his life. Instead of losing confidence, a man with the grace of God can fix these mistakes, which in turn will boost his confidence in God's given abilities. We need to keep in mind that a mistake is not final unless we refuse to correct it. Always remember that those who are confident have a story behind them inspiring them to reach this level of prudence and confidence. By correcting mistakes, you learn from them and convert them to cornerstones of confidence.

Meditation is the remedy for lack of confidence. *In Christ Meditation* brings us to the recognition of the living of the Divine wisdom and power within. The recognition of this marvelous fact is the endorsement of great confidence. The truth that God lives in us and we are the sons and daughters of God through Christ inspires us to splendid levels of confidence. The affirmation *In Christ, I Am Confidence* annuls any negative thought or energy that the Adversary continually tries to feed into our minds. These thoughts and energy are the hidden manipulation of humans' lack of assurance. Meditation on confidence is the beginning of gaining an assertive personality. It is the personality of confidence; it is the personality that is needed for success and achievement. When meditation is mastered in practice, we will gain the personality of confidence, which in turn will be the foundation of another level of success and achievement. When we gain the personality of confidence, we will handle our daily duties with the attitude that there is Divine power working with us and through us. We will act with accuracy and will make the proper decisions in the right time.

(3) Gentleness

Gentleness is one the fruits of the Holy Spirit. "But the fruit of the Spirit is love, joy, peace, longsuffering, kindness, goodness, faithfulness, gentleness, self-control" (Galatians 5:22-23). Gentleness is the character of spiritually and mentally strong people. It is a precious trait. Some are driven by their emotions and some are driven by thoughts of others, which in turn make their behaviors harsh and tough. A gentle person is one whose spirit is the commander and whose mind is the operator. He receives his gentleness from the Holy Spirit within. Hence, he pursues only gentle thoughts, which in turn are reflected in his actions and reactions. He only acts and reacts in a gentle manner.

A dear acquaintance used to have disagreement very often with his wife on any trivial thing. His spiritual mentor advised him to practice gentleness. Of course, this man found it hard at the beginning. One day when his wife was cleaning the china, she accidently broke a precious piece. Instantaneously that man found this incident a good opportunity for what he was practicing - gentleness. For those who like to collect precious china, losing or breaking even part of their collection can be a big deal. His wife expected him to be upset. He told his wife, "It is okay; we have other collections." The funny part is that his wife thought that there was something wrong with him because he was not upset as usual. A few days later, his wife asked him, "Are you okay? Is there anything wrong with you?" "Why?" he asked. "You are not upset." "Being upset will not retrieve what we lost. Let us keep our peace," he replied. That man found his way to exercise gentleness.

Gentleness is one of the most needed traits in dealing with others. We always remember this golden biblical rule, "And just as you want men to do to you, you also do to them likewise" (Luke 6:31). The rule is the foundation to treat others as we would like to be treated, to love them as we want to be loved, and to care for them as we want them to care for us. It is the motivation to be the initiator of kindness and gentleness. However, we don't always encounter receiving kindness and gentleness in return. This is especially so with those who are used by the devil to behave in a way different than Christ wants us to behave. Dealing with those people can be a challenge. Now if you are treating people nicely, but they don't treat you nicely in return, then treat them as God is treating you. As God is treating us with gentleness, so we ought to treat His people. As we are sons of God, we consciously gain Christ-like character. Through Christ-like character, we treat people with love and gentleness greater than with their unkindness. Then we may be a lesson in their lives and they will change. If they do not change, God will keep His sons and daughters spiritually and mentally safe from such people. "You shall hide them in the secret place of Your presence from the plots of man; You shall keep them secretly in a pavilion from the strife of tongues" (Psalm 31:20). It is vital not to adopt anyone's unkind, negative behavior and treat them as they are treating us. Dealing with people in a gentle manner while keeping our spiritual standards is the great manifestation of proclaiming our sonship to God, the Sole Source of gentleness.

In Christ, I Am Calmness and Confidence; I Am Gentleness is the comprehensive affirmation for both our inner being and outer expression of Christ-like character. Calmness is the state of tranquility and silence. In that silence we are able to experience and enjoy the living of Christ in us. Then through the grace and the help of the Holy Spirit, we are able to unfold gentle thoughts from within. In turn our deeds will be expressions of our gentleness. When we become conscious of the power of our thoughts, we will only pursue pure and gentle thoughts, and so we will have a good and peaceful life.

15: In Christ, I Am Compassion and Forgiveness. I Am Mercy.

(1) Compassion

God is infinite compassion. If we would like to describe compassion, we will end by describing God Himself. It always astonishing the immeasurable compassion of Christ. He called to Himself all sinners, the tax collectors, and the sick people with compassion that is sometimes beyond our human expression to describe. "Son, be of good cheer; your sins are forgiven you" (Matthew 9:2). The Lord is calling the paralytic man "son" even before his sins are forgiven. This is the absolute compassion of Christ. His compassion made Him to go to all the cities and villages, preaching the gospel of the kingdom, and healing every sickness and disease among the people. This is because He was moved with compassion for all people.

Since Christ is the same and He will never change, His compassion is never changed. Through Christ's compassion, He allows those who do not know Him, or know Him but reject Him, to succeed and prosper. This is the absolute compassion of God and the free will that He granted every human on earth. Through His compassion, He waits for the ungodly to repent and come back to Him. This is His love, longsuffering, and compassion. Sometimes we wonder how He allows prosperity for those who reject Him. This thought has come to people who dealt closely with God from early history. The Psalmist David had the same thought and said, "For I was envious of the boastful, when I saw the prosperity of the wicked" (Psalm 73:3). If there is a word to express this dealing of God with such people, it is compassion. Now the challenge arises when the devil uses some people who do not know God, denying His presence, and yet are successful.

The intent of the Adversary is to distract sons of God from the Father. By all means, we do not want to use or abuse God's compassion as some do. God has unique ways of dealing with each one of us to compassionately bring us back to Him.

One face of compassion is extending sympathy to others who are entrapped by certain ungodly behaviors. Compassion is the immeasurable characteristic of God. Because of God's compassion for us, He forgives our sins and covers them. Now if God forgives us and covers our sins, we ought to do the same with each other. While doing so is a great wisdom, we still need to pray for each other, so that those entrapped by certain behaviors can find the right way. No one has the intention to make mistakes or live in sin. It is the devil who entraps our brothers and sisters, then also tempts us to judgmentally talk about them.

Contrary to compassion, the devil succeeds in making some of us talk about the bad behavior of others and feel that we ourselves are perfect. Such talk about their behavior of others is defaming their reputation. A wise man taught me this concept: revealing the behavior of others is equivalent to putting mud on their reputation. Now let us imagine that physically you hold mud to put on that person. You have to hold it first with your hand. Then the conclusion is that you have made your hand dirty before you even reach the other person. So, by all means, when we reveal the person's behavior, we are defaming ourselves first. We are telling others that we are judgmental. We are not forgiving. We do not have compassion.

When we are tempted to reveal the bad behavior of others and not to show compassion, remember that someone else will reveal our behavior as well. Also, we may be tempted by the same temptation. We need to remember these two verses: "And just as you want men to do to you, you also do to them likewise" (Luke

6:31). "For whatever a man sows, that he will also reap" (Galatians 6:7). It is wisdom to remember that if you want to correct this man, do it privately between you and him. This will bring positive outcomes. The most important thing is to pray for that person, and God will correct this person from his deeds. In this way, we can use the same time that we would've wasted in talking about others in meditation.

As all humans are created to be sons and daughters of God, in Christ, there is compassion in every one of us. God is the Whole, Absolute compassion, and we are relative compassion that is a part of His compassion. The question is, where is this compassion? Or how can this compassion within us be revived? The devil has succeeded to make this compassion go and fade away from us as humans. He started with people who have hardships and tough conditions, and suggests to them that there is no compassion on earth in these days. If these people do not have a solid biblical spiritual foundation, they start to deal with others in uncompassionate ways. The result is that uncompassionate attitudes have become a contagious illness in our day.

In Christ, I Am Compassion is the antidote for the widespread illness of an uncompassionate attitude. The more we recite this kindhearted affirmation, the more we ingrain in our subconscious that we are the extension of Christ's compassion on earth. When we meditate on Christ's compassion, we are recognizing His compassion in our lives. As we discover how Christ is compassionate with us, we show compassion to the ungodly, the distorted, the rejected, the despised, and all people around us. The more we show compassion and empathy to others, the more we live Christ and they see Him in us. Hence after, people will leave their ungodliness and straying ways to walk in the path of Christ's compassion too.

(2) Forgiveness

Christ came to earth to forgive us our sins and save us from the bondage of the enemy. The core of Christ's mission on earth is forgiveness, deliverance, and healing. When we understand Christ's mission, we as sons and daughters of Christ, come into knowing that forgiveness is a necessity for a healthy spiritual life. On the contrary, unforgiveness is the basis for divisions and distortions in our lives, and these are from the devil. Certainly, unforgiveness is not from Christ! Without forgiving, we cannot receive forgiveness from the Father (Matthew 6:15). Without forgiveness, our prayers are not accepted (Mark 11:25). We can only live as sons and daughters of God when are forgiving ourselves and others as well. However, this is not the scenario seen most in our daily life. The devil entraps some of us in an unforgiving attitude, then portrays to us that God is not forgiving us as well.

Most of the time people have this temptation that God is not forgiving when they are faced with life challenges such as financial hardships, marital or family strife, or illness. They may have some sort of guilt about sins they have committed in the past. They may have repented, but it is among the enemy's tactics during difficult days to remind them of these transgressions.

A dear friend began to face hardships in his career. Things were not going well the way he had anticipated. He quit his job and could not find other employment. He was in the process of getting more education and certain certification that would qualify him for new work. The devil was trying to entrap that man in doubt of God's forgiveness for his past sins. Through the guidance of the Holy Spirit, this man agreed to write down God's blessings in his life, and wrote a few pages listing God's gifts and provision. The amazing thing is that after he finished writing out these blessings, this man no longer needed affirmation that God forgave all his past sins. After a few discussions, he realized he had to ask the Lord for forgiveness as well as forgive people who had caused him pain in his life, and he did so. In this way, he will not succumb to this trap again. Currently, he is a very successful, forgiving person.

It is not we who do not want to forgive others, it is the devil who entraps our minds in such an attitude. In the study and analysis of human behavior, I found that every man has the tendency to forgive. However, the devil keeps reminding us of events from the past, words said by others to offend or that offended even though the speakers may not be conscious of what they said. As the devil works continuously to influence us not to forgive and be hostage to unforgiveness, we need a remedy to counter this battle. The absolute remedy is meditating on forgiveness.

In Christ, I Am Forgiveness is the proclamation of Christ's forgiveness in our lives and the lives of others around us. If Christ is forgiving us, we ought to forgive others. If we would like to live as sons and daughters of God, and if we would like to live as Christ-like persons, we must forgive. We must forgive ourselves and forgive others. *In Christ, I Am Forgiveness* is the affirmation that we are living and acting with forgiveness no matter what the enemy is telling us, no matter what the adversary pushes in our way, and no matter what happened in the past. When we meditate on forgiveness, we will recognize and comprehend God's forgiveness in our lives. When we meditate on God's forgiveness, we will truly find out that "He has not dealt with us according to our sins, nor punished us according to our iniquities" (Psalm 103:10). Not only does God forgive our unrighteousness, but He also forgets it. "For I will forgive their iniquity, and their sin I will remember no more" (Jeremiah 31:34).

(3) Mercy

Mercy is God's innate Divine character to forgive us and to have compassion on us. God's mercy is the expression of His forbearance until we repent. Through His mercy, He overlooks our transgressions; He sends His sun every day on both the good and the evil persons. God's mercy is bigger than any sin. It is greater than the sins of the whole world. God's mercy is endless toward man. "Through the Lord's mercies we are not consumed, because His compassions fail not. They are new every morning; great is Your faithfulness" (Lamentations 3:22-23).

Many years ago in the summer, I went to the beach with my friends. As we were in the water enjoying the jump and the waves, we kept saying, "Thank God the weather is so nice today." Another friend said, "The water is clear; it is a perfect day to be on the beach." The tone of our talk was praising God for the good weather and the nice time that we were spending. A moment later I heard a man close by say, "Hallelujah." "Hallelujah, praise God," I replied. That man was a giant and his body had many scars. At first, I was reluctant to enter into conversation with him, but as we did chat, within minutes he shared all he had done in his life. He kept saying, "Hallelujah, Jesus saved me." In his youth, he travelled to another country where he got involved in a gang. He committed every kind of sin that a man might know. He told me that Samson had one Delilah, but he had many. The scars were from gunshots that he survived. I got chills not from the weather or the water, but from what I was hearing. Somehow, while he was in prison, this man had been introduced to the Bible. Then many miracles happened with him. Only through God's mercy did He escape that gang. He left that country. He became Christian; he repented. He stated that the devil always tries to remind him of his past and make him give up this new life. However, he believes that God's mercy cleansed him. One of the amazing things he mentioned was that Christ knew all his sins when He was upon the cross. It is God's mercy that saved him.

God's mercy is greater than all the sins of all humans in all ages since the beginning of the creation to the end of ages. If the devil makes you think that your sins are greater than God's mercy, this is a trap of despair. Trust and believe that God's mercy is bigger than any sin. This includes all sins that a person has committed, commits, or will commit. This also includes the sins of the whole world. God's mercy led many to repentance until they became great examples for us, even historical figures such as St. Augustine and St. Frances of Assisi. History states that many have gone astray and committed sins, yes, even grave mistakes, yet have repented. If God changed them, He can change any of us as well. If you are troubled by your sins and mistakes of the past and you are in the path of repentance, remember to pray with the Psalmist, "Purge me with hyssop, and I shall be clean; wash me, and I shall be whiter than snow. Create in me a clean heart, O God, and renew a steadfast spirit within me" (Psalm 51:7,10).

Mercy is one of the fundamental teachings of Jesus Christ in the Beatitudes. "Blessed are the merciful, for they shall obtain mercy" (Matthew 5:7). We are only able to live in Christ's mercy when we meditate on His mercy. We are only able to manifest Christ's mercy in our lives and the lives of others around us when our spirits are in direct rapport with Christ, the Spring of Endless Mercy to all humans, including the sinners, the deceivers, hypocrites and those who reject Him. When we recite the affirmation – *In Christ, I Am Mercy*, mercy will be established in our subconscious mind. Reciting *I Am Mercy* is the proclamation that we are part of Christ's mercy. *In Christ, I Am Mercy* is the safeguard from the continual traps of the enemy to be unmerciful to our brothers and sisters in humanity. When mercy is ingrained in our subconscious mind, we will strive to keep clear connection between our spirits and Christ. Only then will our spirits feed upon Christ's mercy, only then will we present mercy to the world, and only then will we live as Christ-like merciful persons in this unmerciful world.

In a deep sense for every man who is tempted by the Adversary's voice but embraced by Christ's forgiveness and mercy, I wrote this poem:

I'll stand by you.
No matter what you did or what you do.
I'll stand by you because I love you and have begotten you.

I'll stand by you when hardships and winds accrue.
These are not for so long but for a few.
I'll stand by you and walk you through.

Whispers in your ear to think you're alone,
but I AM with you.
You stumble down, but look up at the blue.
You'll see Me standing by you when you change your view.

My forgiveness and mercy are for you.
Repentance you need, and this is true.
My grace is upholding you to make you new.

Time to wake up and take charge of your life queue.
Time to rise up and know what you can do.
I AM with you; you can do more than what you think
you can do. I gave you a clue.

16: In Christ, I Am Prosperity. I have Abundance. I Am Kindness.

(1) Prosperity

Most of us think that prosperity depends on outer conditions and external circumstances. Many of us have our mental power chained by beliefs that prosperity is allocated to certain people. Those who have these beliefs exclude themselves from being prosperous by their own thinking and false beliefs. Others believe that prosperity is inherited from the parents, and that a prosperous father and mother will beget a prosperous son. Although we may recognize that some entertain such beliefs, these ideas don't actually have to do with being prosperous or not. These are the devil's lies. Those who believe this way have allowed these lies to land in their minds then acted upon them.

The Sole Source of prosperity is God Himself. When man recognizes the living of God within, that man will prosper no matter what opposition he encounters in his life. Will God be affected by conditions or circumstances? Certainly not! It is man's freedom from the devil's lies and untrue concepts that makes him to prosper. It is ultimately man's awareness of God living within that brings man to prosperity. Being with God is the core secret of prosperity and success. This secret made an Israelite who was sold as a slave by his brothers to prosper in the foreign land of Egypt. "The Lord was with Joseph, and he was a successful man" (Genesis 39:3). The fact that God was with Joseph made his master recognize the secret of his prosperity. Hence, Joseph found favor in the sight of his master.

Meditation on prosperity will inspire and steer us to prosper. To be inspired, we have to be in the spirit. In the spirit, we see prosperity happening according to God's will. Then through faith, prosperity is actualized from the realm of the spirit to our visible world. To be in the spirit, we have to keep our minds occupied with the word of God. Meditation on the word of God keeps us in the spirit. God revealed the secret of prosperity to Joshua. "You shall meditate in it day and night, that you may observe to do according to all that is written in it. For then you will make your way prosperous, and then you will have good success" (Joshua 1:8). Prosperity is the result of meditating on God's word and living according to His commandments.

Now the world-wide misunderstanding is that prosperity is big bank accounts, luxurious houses, a yacht, and expensive cars. While this is the thought of many, this does not represent the true meaning of prosperity. The true meaning of prosperity is that man will be successful in whatever he does. "But his delight is in the law of the Lord, and in His law he meditates day and night. He shall be like a tree planted by the rivers of water, that brings forth its fruit in its season, whose leaf also shall not wither; and whatever he does shall prosper" (Psalm 1:2-3). We need to give full attention to the phrase "whatever he does shall prosper." Prosperity in one's personal life is having Christ at the center of your life, which is the core and underlies all godly success in life. Prosperity in marriage is having a happy marriage based on understanding, honesty, love, and caring. Prosperity in raising children is raising children in the fear of the Lord and His righteousness. Prosperity in business is providing the best quality of services and having a brilliant reputation among one's counterparts and clients, and in the specialty of the business.

Understanding that the true meaning of prosperity is not about material possessions comes from the word of God. Read what Paul the Apostle says, "For the love of money is the root of all evil: which while some coveted after, they have erred from the faith, and pierced themselves through with many sorrows" (1 Timothy 6:10). The Adversary entraps some of us to work long hours to increase possessions with the thought that this is prosperity. Then, during these long hours spouses and children are left behind. All the while, man's spirit is groaning and his body needs rest. What an empty profit for that man who thinks he is prosperous but loses his soul, marriage, and children (Mark 8:36).

As we, children of God, realize the true meaning of prosperity, we will know it is the Lord's blessing that makes man successful in every aspect of his life. As we discover the Divine resources within, we show forth the Divine blessings in our outer world. No one can manifest prosperity in his life while thinking of failure or lack. *In Christ, I Am Prosperity* is the way to discover the Divine resources within. The affirmation *I Am Prosperity* is the assertion that makes the meditator believe he will in fact prosper because God is within him. *In Christ, I Am Prosperity* makes us proceed and succeed in every aspect of our lives. *In Christ, I Am Prosperity* means I will be successful in all I do because Christ is within me.

In Christ, I Am Prosperity indicates that I do all things with the help of Christ who dwells in me; hence, I am successful. I prosper in my spiritual rapport with God and serving Him, I prosper in my marriage, I prosper in raising my children, and I prosper in my career. When we perfect our meditation on the true meaning of prosperity, we manifest prosperity in our personal lives, marriages, raising children, and jobs. The more we focus our mental power on God's prosperity, we will prosper in earthly matters as well as spiritual matters. "Let the Lord be magnified, Who has pleasure in the prosperity of His servant" (Psalm 35:27).

(2) Abundance

Abundance is the result of prosperity. A prosperous man will always have abundance. That abundance can be abundance of peace, wisdom, joy, patience, righteousness, calmness, confidence, and faith. Abundance of good days with the family. Abundance of understanding of our children and our spouses. Abundance of good memories and relaxed, restful days. Abundance of strong spiritual principles and good morals that cannot be shaken by the turmoil of this world. Abundance of memorized biblical verses that make our minds fortified. One of the main reasons that Christ came to earth is that we would have abundance. "... I have come that they may have life, and that they may have it more abundantly" (John 10:10). Those who don't have abundance did not allow Christ to come into their lives to have abundance. He is willing to give abundance to everyone who trusts in Him.

As with prosperity, most of us think of abundance as multiple bank accounts and plenty of money. While this is the thought of many people, it is not true. We all know that money can give the bed, but cannot give the peaceful sleep. Money can give the most delicious food, but it cannot give the appetite to eat it. Money can afford us the medication and the health insurance, but it does not provide the cure. As sons and daughters of God we have Christ, who can provide us more than what we need and more than what we even think, more than what money can provide. "Now to Him who is able to do exceedingly abundantly above all that we ask or think, according to the power that works in us" (Ephesians 3:20). Even the thought of needing Christ as a source of material abundance is not needed. We need to shift our thought to the level of knowing Christ. We need to elevate our thoughts to the abundance of His knowledge, to the abundance of His power, and to the abundance of His grace.

As now we realize that abundance is not about material possessions and earthly matters, we need to recognize the secret of abundance. Consider the law of action-reaction in our daily life. We say "hi" to whoever says "hi" while walking on the sidewalk or in the work place. We smile at whoever smiles at us. It is a very simple social rule that we live by on a daily basis, and most of us recognize it on the human level. Let us raise up our thoughts, taking this concept and live it with God, the Father. What will be the reaction of the Lord toward our action of blessing Him at the beginning of our day? Of course, He will bless us more abundantly beyond what we think or ask for. *Imagine* that you wake up in the morning and instead of being busy with the daily new tasks and the business agenda, you start your day by blessing God. Then *imagine* God sitting on His throne from heaven looking and asking His angels, "Who is blessing Me? It is a busy world, who remembered Me?" Then the angels say, "It is Your son and he is praising Your name." The Lord will say to His angels, "As he blessed Me, go and bless him and protect him in his way. I send on him abundance of peace, wisdom, joy." There are many Scriptures that we can include in our morning prayers that will express our blessings and praising to God, "Bless the Lord, O my soul; and all that is within me, bless His holy name!" (Psalm 103:1). It is remarkable that the Psalmist blessed God in many of his Psalms. Then, from the abundance that he had in his life, he reminded himself not to forget God's benefits. David abounded in abundance because he learned to bless God.

In Christ, I Am Abundance is the assertion that we have abundance of knowing and the living of Christ within. When we meditate on Christ and His teachings, we will have abundance of peace, wisdom, joy, patience, righteousness, calmness, confidence, and faith. Even if we have material needs, He will provide them to us. He knows what we need even before we ask. He will satisfy our need according to His riches in His perfect ways and time.

(3) Kindness

Kindness is sharing of abundance and prosperity. Kindness is the tendency to give. Kindness is the implied thanksgiving to God for all His blessings by giving and sharing with others. Kindness is giving back God's blessing to Him through sharing His blessings with His creation.

The Lord God teaches us a major concept, that is, being kind to the poor. In the Bible, King Solomon says, "He who has pity on the poor lends to the Lord, and He will pay back what he has given" (Proverbs 19:17). Now it is remarkable to notice the phrase "lends to the Lord." It means that in every poor man Jesus is hidden. And when we give to that poor man, we are giving to Jesus Himself. Isn't this awesome? The deeper core of this concept is that we are not giving anything to the poor from ourselves, but from God Himself. This is because God is the One who gives us the strength to work, to earn, and to have. Now when we give to the poor, the Lord will reward you, "Blessed is he who considers the poor; the Lord will deliver him in time of trouble" (Psalm 41:1). Please notice the word "blessed". It means the pouring out of God's grace upon you. We are blessed because we have merciful hearts. We are blessed because we follow His commandments. These are straightforward blessings. However, there is a greater blessing than this, a bonus one. The bonus is that the Lord will deliver you from troubles. These troubles can be anything and anywhere. They can be troubles at work, at home, or on the road. And who wouldn't want that safeguard? The open expression of being delivered from troubles is to be kind to the poor.

Despite the fact that we can have good hearts toward the poor people we meet, we have to define what is meant by "the poor". Most of us miss and cannot recognize the poor in our daily lives because of our routines and busy life styles. As we are sons and daughters of God, we have to be focused and intentional to recognize the poor and not miss a chance for kindness.

First: the poor could be a person who needs a job and you have a position available in your work place. He is poor because he does not have what you have. If he has the education and qualifications for the job, your kindness is to help this person to apply for the job and offer some resources that will help him. Lack of a job is a lack of finances. Lack of a job can reflect a lack of identity. Lack of a job is an implied need. Helping that man fulfill these shortages is an expression of kindness. Second: the poor can be one of your classmates who does not have the ability to type the class notes as fast as you can, and he needs your notes to succeed. He is poor because he is lacking this ability that you have. Sharing your notes with him is equal to giving to the poor. The majority of us take the attitude that everyone should depend on himself and is capable to study. Out of a good heart, helping those who are stumbling in the class is equivalent to giving to the poor. Blessed you are when you share your God's given abilities with others. The grace of God will bestow upon you. Third: the poor can be a person with low self-esteem or depression, who is constantly being tempted by the Adversary with negative thoughts. These negative thoughts torment him to the end that the man is lacking for sleep and peace. You are rich in good and positive thoughts. Sharing with this person God's inspiration and uplifting him with your good words is equal to giving to the poor. Helping that man to restore his peace and tranquility is giving to the poor, which is another perspective of kindness. Fourth: the poor can be a person who is sick. Those who are sick cannot function normally in life, perhaps cannot run their errands, and may need help. Giving those people some of your time is a great help to them. Providing those people with resources on how to function and manage their life facing the challenges of their illness is a great help. Fifth: the poor can also be the typical picture of the poor; that is, a person on the street who is lacking food, clothing, and shelter. While it may seem obvious that these people need financial help, we must use wisdom and discretion when giving. Some of these people may have gotten to this point as a result of alcoholism, drug abuse, or other negative behaviors. Some of us have the thought that giving money to them will not solve their problems; they may use that money to buy beer or drugs and still be hungry and cold. This might be true, but as kind sons and daughters of God, we can give food or clothes. In addition to these, we can also give them Bibles. Maybe one day they will be responsive to the Lord's message, and they will change. Our kindness to these people will impact them regardless who they are, how they became poor, or whatever their circumstances. We always need to remember that *Kindness is the language that the deaf can hear and the blind can see.*[11]

In Christ, I Am Kindness is the proclamation that will open our eyes to our surroundings and find those who need our help. Meditation on kindness will make us see the shortages in peoples' lives and try to fulfill them with God's given blessings. "The poor" is not only that man on the street who wants a couple of dollars. The poor is beyond that mere definition. When we give and share our blessings, the Lord will multiply our blessings many-fold until we are satisfied beyond that we can measure. As a result, Christ will protect us and keep us safe from troubles. *In Christ, I Am Kindness* is the affirmation that inspires us to be a cheerful giver. A cheerful giver is the one who gives out of a heart filled with joy knowing that all is from God and to God, and we are just messengers of giving. The world needs our kindness to treat the illness of being unloved. *There are many medicines and cures for all kinds of sicknesses. But unless kind hands are given in service and generous hearts are given in love, I do not think there can ever be a cure for the terrible sickness of feeling unloved.*[12]

In Christ, I Am Prosperity. I have Abundance. I Am Kindness.

Meditation on kindness will bring us to apply Christ's teaching, "Give to everyone who asks of you" (Luke 6:30). Being kind to others will reflect that kindness back to us by the Divine Providence, "The generous soul will be made rich, and he who waters will also be watered himself" (Proverbs 11:25). Meditation on kindness will make us understand the paradox that it is more blessed to give than to receive. Yes, this is a true principle, *for it is in giving that we receive.*[13] The word "give" includes money, knowledge, time, effort, resources, and all sorts of help to those who are in need. God bless you. Now the ironic but true fact is that those who learn this paradox and live it give but never care about receiving back.

17: In Christ, I Am Comfort and Healing. I Am the Solution.

(1) Comfort

The striving of human beings is for comfort. The world is constantly in a state of distress. This distress is ultimately because of the influence of the Adversary, "The whole world lies under the sway of the wicked one" (1 John 5:19). It is terrible that in our day humans not only feel distressed, but they manifest stress in all aspects of their lives. They speak of stressful jobs, life events, health, and TV shows. They repetitively magnify the negatives and the challenges until life becomes stressful. The ironic thing is that only some of us spend time in observing human behavior and life analysis to find out the underlying cause of these distresses.

As sons and daughters of God, it is our input in the world that provides comfort in our surroundings. However, we are only able to provide comfort to others when we have comfort in ourselves. We will only have comfort in ourselves when we recognize the Holy Spirit within us. We are the dwellings of the Holy Spirit. The Holy Spirit is the Sole comfort for our souls. The Holy Spirit through us provides comfort to those who need it. The Lord Jesus Christ says, "But the Helper, the Holy Spirit, whom the Father will send in My name, He will teach you all things, and bring to your remembrance all things that I said to you" (John 14:26). The Holy Spirit is the Spring of comfort and help within in us.

We all need the Holy Spirit to teach us how to function in our lives. Distress happens as the world is under the sway of the wicked one. We need the Helper, the Teacher, and the Comforter who teaches us how to deal with every aspect of our lives.

The Holy Spirit will teach us how to deal with our spouses, children, parents, in-laws, coworkers, neighbors, and friends. He will tell us to go away from this scornful fellow; He will teach us how to spend time with these godly people because they will help to impart wisdom and to raise our spirits. He will tell us what we have to do and when to do it. He will teach us to do the right thing at the right time. He will teach us when to speak and what to say; hence, our words will be gentle and inspiring to the hearers. He will teach us when we should be silent, and that silence will be equated with deep wisdom. He will guide us to what college or university we should attend, and what major we should study. He will teach us which career we should choose. He will teach us how to overcome obstacles in our lives as we encounter them. He will teach us how to correct mistakes we have made before self-awareness and spiritual awakening. He will tell us what is good food for our health. He will tell us who is the right spouse to marry. He will tell us the pitfalls in our lives that we need to fix. Dear friend, watch carefully: the phrase "all things" does not leave anything out. We have the Help that we need inside of us, the Help that you and I and everyone in the world are looking for.

The Holy Spirit will teach us all things when we read the word of God. The word of God is what the Holy Spirit uses to provide us with the right Scripture at the right time. Now, the more room we free in our heart for the Holy Spirit, the more room He will fill in. The more room He fills in, the more He will guide our life. The more He will guide our life, the more we are able to discern the influence of the Adversary and reject his temptation. The more we reject the enemy's temptations, the more we have God's comfort in our lives.

In Christ, I Am Comfort is acknowledgment that we are the temple of the Holy Spirit. Meditation on His comfort will give us comfort in ourselves and will cause us to manifest comfort to others. The proclamation *In Christ, I Am Comfort* will bring us as sons and daughters of God to be the comfort that the world is looking for. When we meditate on comfort, we can provide comfort. *I Am Comfort* make us channels of the Holy Spirit to all those who need peace, sympathy, and relief in their lives. There is deep yearning in every one of us to comfort each other, and meditation on Christ's comfort will bring us to fulfill this need.

(2) Healing

The need for healing has arisen from the fact that pain and illness have visited most of inhabitants of earth. Illness has taken different forms and periods in people's lives. Some illnesses are physical, some are mental, and some are spiritual. While some illnesses are temporary, some are for long periods and may even be for life. The worst illness is the spiritual one; that is, the disconnection of man from God.

A man who is disconnected from God feels helpless while facing even a trivial illness. A man who recognizes that God lives within has hope while facing a serious illness. If so, then healing begins from the recognition of the living God within. God through His unconditional love manifests Himself to every man. When man accepts Christ, he is a son of God. Once man recognizes this simple fact, a door of endless hope opens in his heart and in his mind. This is the spiritual healing. Once this healing is established the healing for all other types of illnesses will follow.

One of the fundamental ministries of Christ on earth was healing. Christ bore our illness and we through His holy sufferings get healed. "But He was wounded for our transgressions, He was bruised for our iniquities; the chastisement for our peace was upon Him, and by His stripes we are healed" (Isaiah 53:5). Healing is an integral part of Christ's salvation. The will of God from the beginning is goodwill toward man, and man to live with Him in perfect relationship as did Adam and Eve in the garden (Genesis 2:8). Disease entered into man's life after the transgression of His commandment, with the result that we lost peace with God, with ourselves, and with creation (Romans 5:12). Through Christ's passion, we are thoroughly healed, and the lost peace restored to us. As Christ went from city to city, He was fulfilling the healing ministry. "When evening had come, they brought to Him many who were demon-possessed. And He cast out the spirits with a word, and healed all who were sick, that it might be fulfilled which was spoken by Isaiah the prophet, saying: "'He Himself took our infirmities and bore our sicknesses'" (Matthew 8:16-17). There is no illness that Jesus couldn't heal, and He heals all who seek Him, submitting to His Divine wisdom and timing.

The frequent question is why are some healed Divinely while others are not? The answer is doubt, which is a tool of the devil. We have seen many people become ill, and their priests, pastors, friends, families, or spiritual mentors say to them, "Pray that God heals you." Then we hear the reply from those who are sick, "Well, if God has permitted this illness why would He heal me?" Or some have the thought that they are sinners and God will not heal them. These are deceptions from the devil sent to hinder Christ's healing ministry. Christ is willing to heal all who are sick (Matthew 12:15). If the devil tells you are a sinner, then repent. This includes confessing your sins, forgiving others and yourself, and release from your mind any guilt or resentment of the past. If the devil makes you doubt, then carefully consider your faith. In whom do you believe? Dwell on the word of God and be attentive to the miraculous healing of Christ. Recite Psalms that will uplift your spirits. Believe that as those people written about in the Bible got healed, you also can be healed as well. Healing can happen today; it can happen at any unexpected time. Anticipate healing and it will happen.

In Christ, I Am Comfort and Healing. I Am the Solution.

Meditation on healing has immense impact on the meditator as well as all his surroundings. The paradox that always amazes me is that God created herbs and chemicals. He created pharmacists who formulate all these together and make tablets and capsules. God created physicians who diagnose and prescribe these medicines. God also created angels of mercy, nurses, to administer these medicines. But where is God? He is in me and you and in every one who is in Christ. Meditation on healing is the shortest way to God's miraculous power from within. It is beautiful that God provided the development of a complete system we now call the healthcare system to help take care of patients. Also, it is wonderful that we see people receive Divine healing. It's called "miracle" because it is unexplained by the human mind. *Miracles are not contrary to nature, but only contrary to what we know about nature.*[14] However, these miracles prove that Christ is still working. Of course, He always is working and always healing people. He is the same today and yesterday and forever (Hebrews 13:8).

In Christ, I Am Healing is the affirmation that empowers our minds as sons and daughters of God that we are the channels of Christ's healing on earth. The healing merely occurs when we present Christ to the ill person. The paradoxical equation that keeps happening, but is rarely ever noticed, is that Christ plus illness equals blessing (Christ + Illness = Blessing). Once an ill person encounters Christ, the healing will happen even if we don't notice physical change at once. Healing may happen through a process, and can have different forms. All that we need to do is present Christ, and the rest is for Him. The encounter with Christ will be the cornerstone of healing and change in that man's life. Meditation on healing leads us to acknowledge these facts. By reciting the affirmation *I Am Healing* we receive healing for ourselves and others. As sons and daughters of God, we pray with those who are sick and Christ will heal them. This is His promise,

"And these signs will follow those who believe: In My name they will cast out demons; they will speak with new tongues; they will take up serpents; and if they drink anything deadly, it will by no means hurt them; they will lay hands on the sick, and they will recover" (Mark 16:17-18). It is our vital duty to call the name of Christ over illness; His name is the name of salvation. Healing and recovery will happen in God's timing. It may happen today or tomorrow. For sure, it will happen. When God says something, He will do it. Heaven and earth pass away, but none of His promises will by any means go unfulfilled (Mark 13:31). Through meditation on healing, we have firm belief in ourselves that we can offer Christ with all His healing powers to others.

(3) The Solution

One major challenge of the world these days is that while there are many problems, there are few solutions. Problems happen and accumulate everywhere: in our houses, in our jobs, in our churches, and on the roads. Ironically and interestingly, there are even problems between a man and himself. Remember, behind every problem is a devil, assigned to entrap and tempt us. The good news is that behind every solution is One, Christ.

There is a great need to shift from thinking and dwelling on problems and start thinking of solutions. The maneuver of the devil is to entrap humans in one problem after another until all get compiled. Sometimes it is a challenge even to find out the root cause of the problems. Too often some of us think that we are solving a problem, while we actually are adding another problem to the current ones. On other occasions, some of us procrastinate making a decision to solve a problem until it is too late.

Some have left division in their houses until divorce resulted. Some refused to correct and change behaviors requested by their spouses until they lost their soulmates. Some have let misunderstanding between them and their children continue until the children got lost and some left the house. Some speak negatives and are pessimistic until the things that they don't want literally do manifest in their lives. Some speak unintentional words that break wonderful relationships and friendships. Some have problems in their jobs as the result of pointing out the negatives and not appreciating what they are doing until they have created resistance and barriers for good performance. Some left their houses and relocated in the name of job promotion while leaving the family alone, and the family fell apart. Some kept talking about problems with ungodly people until the first problem got doubled. Some have refused to follow advice from parents and grandparents; words which were grace messages from God to them. Regardless the different types of problems, the root cause remains the Adversary of the humans.

There is no problem without a solution except for those which are not submitted in front of Christ. Once we submit our problems to Christ, He is faithful and willing to solve them. The starting point of any solution is the reconciliation of man with God. Once a man is in rapport with God, then all the solutions are available. To reconcile with God, man needs to sit with himself and ponder his thoughts, actions, and reactions according to the Scripture. Man reconciling with God is the fundamental solution. God is in every man who is in Christ. Man reconciling with himself is first reconciling with God within. As man is at peace with himself and God within, he is awakening Christ in the ship of his life. Then Christ will settle the storms and the winds in man's life. Christ is the solution for every problem.

Meditation on solution will shift our thinking from problems to the solutions. *In Christ, I Am the Solution* is the affirmation that has many positive implications. *In Christ, I Am the Solution* implies that Christ in me is the solution for every problem. Christ will provide me with a solution for issues that I encounter. *In Christ, I Am the Solution* means that I present Christ to whoever has a problem and He will provide the solution. My role is just to present Christ. *In Christ, I Am the Solution* steers the mind to the living concept – what would Jesus do? *In Christ, I Am the Solution* shifts the mind from being anxious; hence, we are able to find a solution. A great deal of not finding solutions is being anxious. *In Christ, I Am the Solution* is the testimony of being anxious for nothing, but to Christ bring everything by prayer and supplication with thanksgiving (Philippians 4:6). *In Christ, I Am the Solution* means that I will do what I am required to do in the workplace and go the second mile. *In Christ, I Am the Solution* implies that I will help my spouse in the house without comparing who does more for the family. *In Christ, I Am the Solution* means that I will be the peacemaker among family members, friends, and acquaintances; I will be the starter to diffusing contention and bring peace. A man who lives in Christ-like character will never be without a solution for any issue he encounters. When we meditate on Christ, the Sole Source of life, problems disappear and all we have left are the solutions.

18: In Christ, I Am Healthy and Wealthy. I have Strong Memory.

(1) Healthy

The life of man's spirit is God and His word; the life of man's mind is pure knowledge, education, and continual meditation on God's word. The life of man's body is healthy food and regular exercise. A well-balanced man is the one who is diligent to sustain them all.

As we have presented that meditation is the magnificent remedy for our spirits and our minds, there is a need to also focus on the health of our bodies. Good health is a state of optimal being that allows us to use our energy to perform our daily tasks. It is ironic that everyone would like to be healthy, but not everyone would like to spend the time to take care of his health. The result then is that instead of time being spent to take care of health, it is spent on illness. The underlying reason for many unhealthy men is weak willpower, which is one of the traps of the devil. While this is true, meditation on willpower is the remedy for us to regain strong willpower. Christ will restore willpower for those who willing to take charge of their lives. It is very interesting that the grocery stores have not left any excuse for us not to eat healthy food, except that man who will not direct himself to the habit of eating healthy food. Varieties of food have included plain, sugar-free, decaffeinated, two percent, fat-free, whole, different flavors, or veggie. As we live in a highly oriented customer service society, food industries have made sure to provide us with wide ranges of food options to satisfy our demands and tastes. It is amazing to see fruits already cut, neatly packaged and ready to eat.

It is fascinating to see salads items ready to be mixed and make healthy side dishes. It is we, not the food, who keep ourselves from being healthy.

It is great that one may exercise. However, the devil has to play his role with those who are active. As they exercise to burn calories, he entraps some of them to replenish the calories that they burn in exercise. The need is to replenish the water that you lost and be hydrated, and not to replenish the calories. If a man replenishes calories after exercise, what is the benefit of the exercise? It is just time wasted.

A frustrated friend talked about trying different things to lose weight and none of them was bringing results. Working out and a different nutrition regime were some of his efforts. Analyzing the situation, this friend did not cut off calories and remained entrapped in eating excessive amount of chocolate.

We become healthy to the degree to which the mind thinks healthy thoughts and the soul is morally clean.[15] Meditation on being healthy is the cornerstone principle for good health. *In Christ, I Am Healthy* empowers us to do the best for our spirits, minds, and bodies to be healthy. The affirmation *In Christ, I have Willpower and I Am Healthy* is the iron intention to empower us for excellent health. If my willpower is weak, I submit to Christ to strengthen it, and then I will do all good things for my health. This is a vital pillar in any achievement. The affirmation *I Am Healthy* is the reminder that I cut calories and have to exercise on a regular basis. Meditation on good health brings us to create time for our health instead of spending time in front of TV, on a cellphone or another device. The assertion *I Am Healthy* is the hard stop for saying, "I eat junk food." The first assertion has positive impact on our minds, while the second sentence declares I am not taking care of my health. Meditation on being healthy will inspire us to learn how to prepare healthy meals and change our eating habits. For example, we can take food with us to work instead of buying prepared foods. This can have double benefits: we are eating healthy and saving money. Those who want to be healthy have no excuse. If one cannot afford going to the gym, then walking around the block will be the alternative solution. It is your decision to change destructive behavior to constructive habits that will empower you with good health and good shape. What we sow is what we will reap. Giving our bodies good food will make us develop healthy bodies. Then if you are healthy, you are wealthy in wonderful way.

(2) Wealthy

Man's wealth has many aspects. As we have seen, man's greatest wealth is to be healthy. One of man's greatest assets is to have an excellent reputation. Wealth is the state of abounding in prosperity; prosperity is to be successful in what one does. The secret of prosperity is abiding in God. As wealth has many aspects, one important aspect of man's wealth is to have sufficiency in everything needed (2 Corinthians 9:8). When man has an excess of financial resources but a lack of health and peace, then this man is far from being wealthy. True wealth is the sufficiency of every aspect of life. Man can have sufficiency when he is rightly connected to God, "Not that we are sufficient of ourselves to think of anything as being from ourselves, but our sufficiency is from God" (2 Corinthians 3:5).

The fundamental secret of being wealthy is obedience in paying the tithe. If wealth, prosperity, and abundance come from God, then paying the tithe is the basic thanksgiving for His gifts. It is not simply we who worked to generate this money and wealth. It is God who gave us the power to work and to succeed. Giving the tithe has three vital implications. First: we are offering thanks to

God for giving us power to work. Second: tithing is a commandment. The Lord says, "Bring all the tithes into the storehouse, that there may be food in My house," (Malachi 3:10). Third: it is a legitimate way to receive more blessings and increase. The Lord in the same verse says, "... try Me now in this...if I will not open for you the windows of heaven and pour out for you such blessing that there will not be room enough to receive it."

A teenager lost his dad while he was in senior high school. Despite the fact that his mom had a stable job, her income was meager to support the finances of the home. One thing the mom never stopped doing in the turmoil of these devastating circumstances was paying the tithe on a regular basis. Not only just paying the tithe, but also paying it from the first check that she earned. A few years later that teenager graduated and got a job and learned to pay the tithe. A few years after that, he faced challenges as he switched between jobs and did not have stable income. Despite this, he kept paying the tithe. He kept God as his first priority; He kept God first in his life. As he continued to be faithful in paying the tithe, the Lord opened for him a door. The Lord guided him to a better career and he found a job with steady income and benefits better than what he had before.

Another aspect of being wealthy is knowing that what you have is enough - a simple fact that many of us miss. There are some people who are blessed with good finances; however, they still need more. Those people do not see that what they have is enough. The devil has entrapped some of us in this spiraling snare. The result is that some run after money to become rich, thinking this is ambition. Ambition is the intense inner flame to achieve a goal and become excellent in something. Running after money can lead to switching jobs frequently and chasing promotions, or working excessive hours and even seven days a week. Chasing money can lead a man astray and to have no peace in his house.

There is a complete difference between healthy ambition and chasing after money. Some people run after money to satisfy unnecessary life expectations thinking this is ambition. The wise advice for avoiding this trap is to remember two things. First: know that what you have is enough. You can adjust your lifestyle to make it enough. Second: by following God's commandments and paying the tithe, He will bless what you have to be enough for your life's journey. "The blessing of the Lord makes one rich, and He adds no sorrow with it" (Proverbs 10:22).

Again, an important aspect of being wealthy is having a good reputation. A man of good reputation is the man of a good name. King Solomon realized this fact a long time ago and stated in the book of Proverbs, "A good name is to be chosen rather than great riches" (Proverbs 22:1). The challenge that most people face these days is that they associate being wealthy with riches and finances rather than with one's good name. A man of good reputation will be trusted by his colleagues and coworkers. A man with a good reputation will be valued by his employer. A good reputation is one intangible wealth a man could have among others. Man's reputation is the recognition of his integrity. One's integrity is the fundamental aspect for having a good name. It is amazing that King Solomon recognized this fact and said, "He who walks with integrity walks securely, but he who perverts his ways will become known" (Proverbs 10:9). A man of integrity is a man with a good reputation. A man with a good reputation will process his life cautiously in order to not lose this great asset. This cautiousness will make him secure. Looking at reputation from a higher perspective, we realize its importance to us as sons and daughters of God. As we are trying to live in a Christ-like manner, we ought to keep our reputation spotless; hence, our reputation is our precious wealth and reflects Christ's excellence.

The mere fact that we have Christ in our lives is the underlying foundation for all wealth. There is no wealth needed beside knowing, believing, and living Christ. The affirmation *In Christ, I Am Wealthy* means that I have the wealth that I need and I do not need more than what I have; I have Christ. It is amazing that those who are wealthy and come to the knowledge of Christ use their wealth to serve God. Zacchaeus the rich man gave up his money after his encounter with Christ (Luke 19:8). He realized the knowledge of Christ is the true wealth. *In Christ, I Am Wealthy* is the shield and guard for any "wealth" traps that come our way. The devil succeeded to sugar-coat worshiping him with the promise of gaining the wealth and glory of the world with the concept of ambition (Matthew 4:9). As Christ did not fall into this trap, we as Christ-like persons ought not to fall into that trap as well. *In Christ, I Am Wealthy* is the protection against false ambition. Meditation on being wealthy is the opening of our eyes that what we have is enough, and whatever is needed will come through God's orchestrated timing. The affirmation of being wealthy is the reminder to pay the tithe on a regular basis. *In Christ I Am Wealthy,* is the reminder of having and keeping our reputation clear. Again, this is one of the greatest intangible assets a man could have in addition to his health. Interestingly, neither a good reputation nor health can be bought by all the money in the world. *In Christ, I Am Wealthy* is the inclusion of all spiritual blessings, that is, grace, joy, peace, patience, wisdom, and tranquility, and not only material possessions.

(3) Strong Memory

Memory is the mental function by which a man can recall certain information and remember certain tasks. In addition to the gift of understanding, memory is another great blessing that God bestowed on us. Both are aspects of true wealth. Memory is the storage of information in man's mind. This which will equip him to perform particular skills based on experience or training.

Healthy minds contain strong memory. Healthy minds are fostered when we control our thoughts, our senses, and are focused. Much of the blessing of a healthy mind is that the peace of God that surpasses everything fills that mind. The first step in attaining a healthy mind is meditating on God's word. Meditating on God's word is the fundamental step to establish the presence of God in man's mind. There is no mind that God lives in that will not be healthy and functioning to the ultimate level.

One of the most mean and strong wars waged by the enemy against us is through memory. Through life observation and analysis, we see the Adversary uses man himself to defeat his memory. This is evident by recalling some common phrases we hear such as, "I do not trust my memory," "I do not remember what I ate yesterday," "I am getting old and my memory is gone." When these phrases come across my ear, I bless the talker, and based on the situation, I tend to remind him that such words can actually make the memory diminish. It is interesting and really ironic that most of those who talk this way can remember certain events and describe them as if they just happened yesterday.

Why does the Adversary war against the wonderful gift of our memory? This is a highly sophisticated strategy. One cruel intention is that a man cannot remember the deeds of the Lord in his life, hence in a weak moment and during hardship may doubt God's love. Some have fallen into this trap and left Christ, resulting in their going astray. Another evil intention is that men may forget the good memories in their lives. The wonderful gift of memory can be refreshing and soothing when challenges arise. The ironic thing is that those same people often remember the negatives and the hardships. If a man can remember negatives and hard days but not the positives and the good days, it means the faculty of memory is working. However, it is misused by the devil against the man himself. In another memory trap of the devil, a man may forget important dates and timelines at work or in the family. By all means there is some evidence that organic disease can affect memory. While medical tests and diagnosis support the evidence, this is not our focus here. We ought to pray and help people who are challenged by these diseases.

In addition to the previously named spiritual war against the memory of our human nature, causing it to be weak, is another spiritual war. Man himself is the dynamic for this second spiritual war. God has blessed some of us with photographic memory. Those who have this blessing know it. The challenge arises when they brag about this blessing. Then the Adversary tempts those people.

A dear classmate was always repeating this sentence, "I have a photographic memory." However, this classmate was getting low grades. If you are a good studier and have excellent memory and do well taking exams, why wouldn't your grades reflect these qualities? This positive and smart person was tempted by the Adversary to keep mentioning her talent. After this classmate joined our study group and accepted the humble advice not to mention this talent, things changed for the better. Through a wise analysis of the classmate's behavior, we realized another pitfall. By continually repeating, "I have a photographic memory" she was tempted by the Adversary to shorten the time of study and to finish exams and leave early without properly reviewing and reasoning the answers. The educational history will not record that she left the exams early, but will indeed record the low grades. Working with the offered simple but wise advice, she started to get high grades and graduated.

In Christ, I have Strong Memory is the antidote for all these traps set by the Adversary against our magnificent memory. Meditation on strong memory make us respect our memory and only say what will positively strengthen it. *In Christ, I have Strong Memory* is the affirmation that will make us remember the deeds of the Lord in our lives. It is the affirmation that empowers the memory to remember the positives and let go of the negatives. It is the needed affirmation to refresh and rejuvenate our memory to function to the ultimate level. *In Christ, I have Strong Memory* means I will remember God's commandments and follow them. *In Christ, I have Strong Memory* is also the supplication that Christ will keep my memory healthy to the last breath of my life. *In Christ, I have Strong Memory* is the meditation that is recited in secret; however, in public there is no need to brag or proclaim about it. It is through humbleness we recognize God's blessings and give thanks to Him, helping others to recognize His given gifts and talents as well.

19: In Christ, I overcome Illnesses and Spirits. I overcome myself. I Am a New (Man, Woman). I Am Christ-like.

(1) Overcoming Illnesses and Spirits

The greatest victory a man can achieve in his life is overcoming evil spirits and himself. The only way to this victory is Christ. Meditation is the recognition of the living of Christ within us; hence, we through Him can overcome evil spirits and ourselves.

There are evil spirits behind every problem and every kind of illness. The true healing of illness is founded on deliverance. As Christ cast out the demon, the mute spoke (Matthew 9:33). And when He cast out a spirit of infirmity, the woman became loosed and immediately was standing up straight after being held bent over for eighteen years (Luke 13:12). As people presented those sick with various diseases to Christ, He laid His hands on every one of them and healed them, and demons also came out of many (Luke 4:40-41). The challenge arises when people don't recognize the existence of these evil spirits. Some of these illnesses come as a direct result and some come gradually.

A man may lose interest in life and quickly be afflicted by depression. It is possible if he doesn't get treated, deeper depression may develop. In other situations, depression might come on gradually. It is vital not to treat or deal with only symptoms, yet leave the causes without treatment. For effective treatment, it is important to know the root cause(s) and the course of events. It is remarkable to understand that there is no illness without healing once it is submitted to Christ.

Through observation and human behavior analysis, we find four characteristics the Adversary sneaks into men's lives, thereafter leaving the door open for many pitfalls. These serious characteristics are arrogance, ignorance, self-sufficiency, and self-righteousness. A man may be affected by one of these, some, or all of them. The challenge is when a man gives place to any of these and does not know that his very life is at risk. It is like a man who's sick and doesn't know he is sick.

Arrogance makes man puffed up about the blessings of God's given gifts and talents. Isn't it God who gave to you these talents, and you did not earn them for yourself? Why are you arrogant? A man can be trapped by arrogance for his title, sophisticated job, successful business, secured career, big bank account, or myriad things real or imagined. Again, isn't it God who gave you the power to proceed and succeed? Humbleness is the remedy for this pitfall.

Ignorance makes a man ignore knowing God and His spiritual laws. Those who ignore God fundamentally deny His existence yet demand proof for His existence. David the Psalmist says, "The heavens declare the glory of God; and the firmament shows His handiwork" (Psalm 19:1). One simple fact that proves God's existence is that through His sovereignty, His absolute accurate might, He sustains the distance between the earth and the sun. If by one millimeter the earth comes closer to the sun, the heat of the sun will burn everything living on it. If by one millimeter the earth goes away from the sun, all living things may perish from the decrease of temperature. When we see a painting, we realize there is a painter that painted it. Those who deny God's existence need to know that there is a Creator that created the universe. Then some recognize God's existence but ignore His spiritual laws because they don't want any restraints. They would like to live their lives according to their carnal desires. They feel that God's

In Christ, I overcome illness and spirits. I overcome myself.

I Am a new (man, woman). I Am Christ-like.

spiritual laws restrict them, so they ignore them. Ignorance is the direct result of not knowing the Scriptures. Studying the Scriptures is the cure for this pitfall.

Self-sufficiency is another snare that the enemy uses to trap some of us. Those who get caught in this trait typically proclaim phrases like, *I am independent. I do not need anyone. I am self-sufficient.* The only sufficiency on our planet is though God's love. Through His love, He lets the sun rise every day. We receive these sun rays, and through the solar system harness forms of energy for our use. We then proclaim that we produced our energy and we call it self-sufficiency. Through God's love, He sends rains on the earth to grow crops and grain. Then some take these grains and produce flour and bake their own bread. Then they think they are self-sufficient. The remedy for this trait is for man to recognize that God created the universe based on love. Through this love He provides for us, everyone provides some sufficiency to others, and others provide some sufficiency for them.

The most notable pitfall is self-righteousness. Those who fall into this may be humble, aware of God's existence and worship Him, and take heed of His spiritual laws. They know that sufficiency is from God. However, they set up certain spiritual rules and practices with the goal to reach God and please Him. Later on, they wander astray from their primary goal. Instead of worshiping God, the goal becomes fulfilling these rituals, which makes them righteous and justified in their eyes. The remedy for this is knowing that justification and righteousness are through faith and are given freely by the grace of God. "For by grace you have been saved through faith, and that not of yourselves; it is the gift of God, not of works, lest anyone should boast" (Ephesians 2:8-9).

Once the Adversary sneaks into a man's life by any of these four traps, he has the door opened for others. Other traps can be lack of self-control, judgment, fear, pessimism, nervousness, illness, laziness, gluttony, bad habits, adultery, hyper-sexuality, unfaithfulness, hatred, bitterness, deception, lying, stealing, confusion, doubt, division, alcoholism, addiction, smoking, procrastination, weakness, violence, depression, murder and suicide – to name only some!

The Adversary works through strategic tactics. He is very organized. This is explained by St. Paul, "For we do not wrestle against flesh and blood, but against principalities, against powers, against the rulers of the darkness of this age, against spiritual hosts of wickedness in the heavenly places" (Ephesians 6:12). He starts with little things; however, the goal is to entrap man's life on earth and in eternity. The gate for all other spirits begins with the lack of self-control. If a man does not practice self-control, this vulnerability can spread to any aspect of his life.

Lack of self-control accompanied with gluttony leads to obesity. If these are added to laziness, then there will be no exercise or workout, and obesity will lead to illness such diabetes, high cholesterol, and heart conditions. Then we seek treatment for the illness and don't recognize the root causes - lack of self-control, gluttony, and laziness.

A student procrastinates studying for an exam with an imaginary thinking that he will focus the night before the exam and get all the material covered. He then becomes nervous the night before the exam and may not study well. Adding lack of self-control to procrastination, the student's mind can wander during studying and the gain will be minimal. The end results are low grades. If this goes on and becomes a pattern and studying style, this student may end up in a career he does not like or is not meant for him. He could be one of the smartest students, but succumbed to lack of self-control, procrastination, and nervousness.

A man starts to drink one beer every night with the thought that it helps in relaxation, stress relief, or winding down. Adding this to lack of self-control, the number of beers will increase gradually and stress will never end. Little by little, this man comes to depend on beer. Later on, he finds himself to be alcoholic with many illnesses. Finally, we see an alcoholic who is drunk and violent. This man could be the most nice and generous person if he was not ensnared by this trap.

A couple lived a peaceful life together for many years. Once they decided to get married and live according to God's ordinance and straighten things out, their lives actually turned upside down. Why? Because they chose to live according God's ordinance of marriage, the devil would now not leave them alone. The devil succeeded in turning this biblical verse, "He who finds a wife finds a good thing, and obtains favor from the Lord" (Proverbs 18:21) to this cultural statement, "Marriage is the beginning of troubles." Now the devil can use tactics such as hyper-intimacy or unfaithfulness, so the same couple who lived together happily for many years, after getting married can fall into temptation and end up getting divorced. These seductions come sometimes in packages, sometimes separately. If both were tempted into hyper-intimacy, then the lust of the body is their god. While they are married to fulfill God's ordinance, they yet can be led astray by their passions if they are not submitted to God. Hyper-intimacy can further develop into fantasies. In this treacherous position of the heart there will be no time for prayer and fasting caring for the things of God. If one of them falls into hyper-intimacy and the one with lower drive always refuses, then unfaithfulness becomes the likely result. Later on, there will be divorce after all hidden things come to light. Of course, there are many other traps the enemy can use, but the conclusion is one: with divorce there are divisions, heart-aches, and devastations. This couple could be the most devoted and faithful ones if they had learned how to secure their marriage.

The challenge that everyone of us faces but not everyone recognizes it is that as long as a man is doing something against God's commandment, the devil causes his heart to grow dull and helps him languish in spiritual hypnosis. Moreover, the enemy lets his life seem successful. Once a man comes to himself and wants to live according to God's commandment, the devil attempts to makes his life a struggle and convinces him that the trials are God punishing him for his past deeds. All this man needs is to be persistent in walking in God's commandments, and the grace of God will sustain him.

Only through repentance and deliverance can a man over-come these evil spirits and the traps of their temptations. We must remember that the whole world is continuously under evil tactics by the Adversary, "We know that we are of God, and the whole world lies under the sway of the wicked one" (1 John 5:19). Failing to recognize this fact makes a man prey for these tactics. Repent-ance is the man's call for help; it is the homecoming of a strayed man unto Christ.

Repentance has steps. First: man needs to determine in his heart that he committed something against God and he doesn't want to do it again. He confesses his sins and asks the Lord to embrace him with His mercy and strength not to come back to any of them. Confessing one's sins brings the grace of God to uplift him into the path of repentance. Through the path of repentance man believes that Christ died on the Cross for his salvation and He is the only way to the Heavenly Father and Eternal Life (John 14:6).

In Christ, I overcome illness and spirits. I overcome myself.

I Am a new (man, woman). I Am Christ-like.

It is the grace of God and the help of the Holy Spirit, that sustain a man not to repeat any of his sins and to walk in the way of righteousness, obeying God's commandments to the last breath. Second: deliverance is the act of Christ towards this man. The best ever fact that Christ showed is that He loves all of us and He wants salvation from sin for all of us. Once Christ delivers a man from the devil's traps, man's heart will be filled with joy and peace. Now this man is in Christ; he is new, and all his sins have been cleansed away (2 Corinthians 5:17). This man must abide in Christ so not to fall again. "Whoever abides in Him does not sin" (1 John 3:6). This man is now under God's grace and sin does not have dominion over him (Romans 6:14). That man will live and declare the great works of the Lord in his life. By giving Christ full control over his life, he will live in continual repentance, enjoying God's grace, virtues, and victory.

In Christ, I overcome illnesses and spirits is the proclamation that we need to recite every day as we become aware of and cautious with all these traps. Those who are entrapped are naïve because they have not known how to secure themselves against these snares. It is only through Christ, the Savior of men's souls, we are able to recognize the traps set against us. It is through the grace of God we can overcome these spirits. Hence, as we overcome these spirits, we avoid and overcome illnesses as well. These illnesses can be mental, physical, or emotional. However, no illness will stand in front of the healing power of Christ.

(2) Overcoming Oneself and Becoming a New (Man, Woman)

It is beautiful that we see and hear many of us would like to change the world. However, not all of those who would like to do so know how. The real change a man can present to the world is the new man in Christ. *You must be the change you wish to see in the world.*[16] It is great wisdom for a man to ponder this simple but important concept. Am I victorious? The true victory and winning a man can achieve is overcoming himself. It is either man being processed by life or a man processing life. As we are sons and daughters of God, we ought to process life. We are called to live life according to what Christ wants us to do.

Overcoming oneself is the victory over all one's carnal desires and sinful habits. Overcoming oneself means carefully considering every thought and every deed. Overcoming oneself means every action and reaction will be with a sense of purpose. Overcoming oneself means mastering oneself for the glory of God; hence after, the true victory. The beginning of overcoming oneself is understanding the underlying cause of sin. Sin is due to the weakness of sinful humanity, as well as to the evil spirits that fight against us. Once our minds understand these facts, our eyes will recognize the works of both our flesh and unseen spiritual beings. Without this recognition and understanding, man will not gain victory. It is vital that a man realizes that in Christ, he is a new creation. When this realization shines in a man's life, he begins to conduct his life as a new man in Christ, and by the power of the Holy Spirit, old traits and carnal desires will be replaced with the fruits of the Holy Spirit (Galatians 5:22-23). Only through Christ a man can overcome himself and become new. "Therefore, if anyone is in Christ, he is a new creation; old things have passed away; behold, all things have become new" (2 Corinthians 5:17). This is the essence of the newness in Christ: a man in Christ can overcome sin and live the life of repentance. A man without Christ cannot overcome sin.

In Christ, I overcome myself is the affirmation that depicts the new creation through the salvation presented by Christ. This assertion means that Christ has erased from me all the vanities of this world (Ecclesiastes 1:14). When this affirmation is established

In Christ, I overcome illness and spirits. I overcome myself.

I Am a new (man, woman). I Am Christ-like.

in our mind and manifested in our life through obedience to God, we will be able to overcome the world. We will perceive the vanities of the world. When we perceive the vanities of the world, and when we focus our eyes on God and His commandments, we overcome ourselves. The real manifestation of a man winning over himself is his submission to Christ; hence, the change of his character. Then, that man will return good for evil, love for hatred, gentleness for ill treatment. That man will remain silent when attacked because he knows that Christ will defend him. That man will be aware of and intentional about thought control and endless improvement. That man will rise up early before the sun rises to consider his daily tasks, and will not be processed by life. That man will meditate on God's word until it sinks deep into his mind and brings fruit in his life. That man will know how to program his mind for success and achievement. That man will be receptive to the grace of God for guidance and how to process his life in a godly manner. A man who overcomes himself will be a Christ-like man. That man will live in God's commandments, fear, love, and righteousness to the last breath. *In Christ, I overcome myself* is the proclamation that *I Am a new man. In Christ, I overcome myself* is declaring one's absolute belief that he has become a Christ-like noble man, filled with and guided by the Holy Spirit.

As a man meditates on and lives out the truth of God's words that give him this declaration *In Christ, I overcome illnesses and spirits. I overcome myself. I Am a new man. I Am Christ-like,* the world will indeed see a Christ-like man.

20: Christ-like Character

In Christ Meditation is the spiritual transformation of oneself into a Christ-like person by the Holy Spirit, for the glory of God, and the sake of our good being. Meditation is building in ourselves spiritual stamina that can overcome the turmoil of the world. It is the practice of establishing a rapport between one's mind and spirit with God. It is the practice that makes us take charge of our mind and receive God's peace. Once we take charge of our minds and they are calm, we will be receptive to the guidance of the Holy Spirit within us. The Holy Spirit always yearns to work in us, but our restless mind is the hindrance in receptivity to His work. Meditation is our intentional reflection on our origin of being, that is God. When meditation is practiced with patience and persistence, the net result is success in our lives and the manifestation of God's power in every aspect of our lives.

Effective meditation starts by recognizing Scriptures for developing solid biblical statements that will be the foundation of transformation. In the previous chapters, we have taken step by step the template that will help us to be Christ-like persons. This template is just the summary of comprehensive biblical verses and Christ's teachings. The template is divided into affirmations. These affirmations are stated in a simple, concise way that is expressed in present tense and personalized, so it can be easily recited using the conscious mind, and readily absorbed by the subconscious mind. The theme of the template is based on the truth that we through Christ are sons and daughters of God. The core value of each affirmation is that we want to live in the world as Christ wants us to. Hence, we become windows for His light into the world and we, through Christ, overcome the world. The affirmations of the template are just starting points. You can add contemplations as you go and as there is need.

However, it is highly recommended to keep the text of the affirmations as the base foundation, and additions can be made verbally. For example, the affirmation of *In Christ, I Am Love; I love God and His creation* can be stated as follows: "*In Christ, I Am Love; I love God* and I love those who offend me." Moreover, you can state here the names of people who offend you. This technique will help you in that when those people come to your mind, you will find yourself blessing them and not talking about them or judging them, which are the intent of the devil. Another example, the affirmation of *In Christ, I have Strong Faith, I trust God; I have no Fear,* can be stated as follows: "*In Christ, I have Strong Faith, I trust God. I have no Fear* and everything will work for my good as I obey God." Another example, *In Christ, I overcome myself* can be stated as follows: "*In Christ, I overcome illnesses and spirits; I overcome myself. I Am a new man.* I overcome my old habits and my old traits." When adding verbal contemplations with personalized meanings to the affirmations, we keep the text short and it will be easier to recite. If it gets too long, it will be a challenge to recite the meditation.

(1) Meditation in Practice

Since meditation results in the transforming of oneself, it is the practice of starting with ourselves. Sit with yourself in a quiet room away from any interruption and interference of the world. At the beginning of this practice it is recommended to sit in front of a mirror while reciting the mediation statements. This technique will help the meditator to reflect on himself. While this is recommended for starting the practice of meditation, some may choose not to do so if this technique will hinder their meditation. The intent of this technique is that looking at one's eyes in the mirror will help a man to be honest in examining and discerning his thoughts. Studying God's words and examining one's thoughts are essential principles to recognize which thoughts are from Christ and which are not. When one sits with himself, he is also sitting with God within. So, sit in a comfortable, relaxed position and recite the positive statements for fifteen to twenty minutes morning and evening every day. You can recite each affirmation multiple times. The intent here is that one faces himself. There may be a great resistance at the beginning. You will feel that you are moving mountains, and this is true. When a man decides to take charge of his mind and live a righteous life in front of God and for His glory, it can seem like moving mountains. Sitting with oneself is the small start that will lead to great change. As sitting with oneself is also intentionally sitting with God within, the devil will tempt the meditator by many various things. These temptations are intended to take man from sitting with God. You may be tempted that there is no time, strength, or motivation. Then find time and catch yourself when you have energy. Ask God for His grace to sustain you in this process. Persevere in practicing meditation for the love of God and for the love of changing oneself to be Christ-like. *Do not be discouraged by the resistance you will encounter from your human nature; you must go against your human inclinations. Often, in the beginning, you will think that you are wasting time, but you must go on. Be determined and persevere in it until death, despite all the difficulties.*[17]

What we contemplate on will become our essence. Gradually, you will notice that the practice of mediation will replace spending your time in whining and worrying about your life. The more you persevere in practicing Christ-like meditation, the more you will see positive changes happening in your life, and the more you will recognize the transformation to Christ-like character. When we feel good about ourselves, people will feel good dealing with us, as well as they will feel good about us. This fact alone offers another motivational starting point of magnificent change whereby we impact our surroundings.

Success comes by organized collaborative work. To gain successful results from meditation, it is needed to practice meditation every day. Practicing mediation twice daily is my routine that helps me toward positive and tremendous results. Gradually, you will find yourself growing in the path of wisdom and self-control. You will find your mind is active but relaxed and can tolerate stress. You will recognize that there is God's Divine power working with you and through you that is His grace. You will feel that you are in a direct rapport with the help of the Holy Spirit from within. You will see polishing in your character. You will be calmer and quieter. As you perfect practicing mediation, you will not only be able to handle stress, but also, you will emit tranquility to diffuse this stress. Stressful conditions and circumstances will be the chance to exercise Christ-like strength. As you succeed in practicing meditation with persistence, you will find your mind being fortified against negatives and you will be able to emanate positive thoughts. You will perceive the presence of God in every circumstance.

(2) Mediation and Prayer

The questions that most people ask are, *What is the difference between meditation and prayer? Can one replace the other? Are they discrete practices?* The answers to these questions are very simple. Meditation is the reflection on God's words and abiding in them by ingraining them in our minds. Prayer is the expressed relationship between man and God. Prayer is the talking to God. Prayer is the seeking to be attentive to God. Prayer has many aspects such as prayer of repentance, prayer for guidance, and prayer of praise and thanksgiving. Meditation cannot replace prayer and prayer cannot replace meditation. Both of these can add to and complete each other. As a matter of fact, meditation can take prayer to a higher level when one recites a certain prayer a few times while praying. Then this prayer becomes meditative prayer.

As I proceeded in practicing meditation, I started to meditate before prayer. At the beginning, I had these two spiritual practices separated. Then, through the guidance of the Holy Spirit, meditation became the warm-up that preceded fervent prayer. In this advanced way, meditation became the reminder that God is my Father, and prayer is talking to Him.

(3) Mediation While Asleep

After years and years of meditation, meditation became the tremendous tool for the most needed change. As the magnificent change started to blossom in my life, there was yet more need of time and effort to meditate. Through prayer, the Holy Spirit guided me to mediate even at night while asleep. Yes, meditation can be at night while asleep. But how and why were questions that needed answers to proceed with this practice.

Seemingly and partially, the answer to the "why" question was that there is more change to be done and this change is desired to take effect in a short time. However, the Holy Spirit guided me as to why at night. At night the enemy often comes and throws evil thoughts into our minds. These thoughts are the seeds for evil action. While we are asleep, we may not perceive it; but it happens. "But while men slept, his enemy came and sowed tares among the wheat and went his way" (Matthew 13:25). These seeds stay in our minds until the proper circumstances then manifest themselves. Most of us have done some actions and wondered why we did what we did, but couldn't find answers. Through the guidance of the Holy Spirit to observe and analyze, the answer is that the devil throws seeds into human minds while they are asleep. Hence the need for meditation to guard our minds even while we are asleep.

As this meditation is composed of affirmations based on verses of the Bible, it is God's words in simplified and selective content. Meditation while asleep is the tuning of one's mind to God's word. At night the conscious mind is asleep but the subconscious is working. Meditation at night is the implied proclaiming that the mind is receptive to God's instruction, "In a dream, in a vision of the night, when deep sleep falls upon men, while slumbering on their beds, then He opens the ears of men, and seals their instruction" (Job 33:15-16).

As the answer for the "why" question was understood, the question for "how" one can meditate at night while asleep also needed an answer. God answers those who ask Him, one way or the other, always with the result being to their benefit. Meditation at night can be understood and practiced by recording these affirmations and listening to them while asleep. When I learned this practice, my life became ever better.

Technology may not be available for all of us and recording of meditation may not be an easy task. When I encounter a counselee challenged by technology, my humble recommendation is to listen to the book of Psalms while asleep. The audio of the Psalms is available on any Bible application. This alternative solution helped many people who couldn't record their personal meditation.

(4) Phases of Mediation

As mediation has become a great blessing from God to me for many years, there are phases that I experienced in my own practice and counseling others in its practice. We always need to remember the ultimate goal of mediation is the transformation of ourselves to Christ-like persons through the grace of God. To be Christ-like persons, we will go through phases that gradually will mold our character to be pure, humble, loving, peacemaking and wise persons, obedient to God. Christ foreknew those who will be receptive and foreordained them to be transformed into the likeness of His Son (Romans 8:29). These attributes can be in variation and relatively accomplished by the perfecting of meditation practice. It is the grace of God that transforms us to the likeness of Christ when we mediate on His words and are receptive to this ever-magnificent transformation.

Resistance Phase: A dear friend, who is facing mostly the same circumstances that I am facing in my daily life asked me about the secret of being calm. My response was simple: to practice meditation. So my friend took the template with instructions on how to meditate. After a few weeks this friend stated that it is impossible to sit in front of the mirror or in a quiet room to recite the meditation or even to pray some Psalms. When this resistance occurs, the underlying factor could be a spirit of lack of self-control or merely laziness. It is a simple fact that it is not Christ who does not want us to be joyous and in charge of our lives. Which one is more beneficial - whining and complaining about your life, or sitting to meditate and intentionally allowing yourself to be receptive to the grace of God to change you? Among the most magnificent results of meditation are becoming better than your present self and living your life as Christ wants for you. This improvement comes by recognizing and accessing the Divine resources God gives through the Holy Spirit. Hence after, changing your mental attitude toward life will change how you process life. Once the meditator recognizes the underlying cause of this resistance, and through the grace of God, he will pass this phase.

Acceptance Phase: Once the meditator passes the resistance phase, he enters another phase that is acceptance. In this phase the meditator admits and accepts that he needs a tool to help himself. He accepts the template, *In Christ Meditation*. Meditators in this phase practice until they start to recognize positive changes in themselves. Some begin to handle stress better. Some feel fresh in the morning after meditation. Some meditators feel energetic after practicing meditation. Despite that all these are initial excellent results, we always need to focus on the ultimate goal of meditation, that is complete transformation into Christ-likeness. Despite that the ultimate goal is not yet reached in this acceptance phase, still those who realize positive change and are able to handle life in a better way, also realize contentment as a result.

Excellence Phase: This phase is achieved when the meditator perceives the need for daily practicing meditation. Based on experience, a meditator enters this phase after many months of practicing meditation with persistence and perseverance. The resulting changes happen gradually in one's life. You will find that you would like to associate yourself with those who like to pursue spiritual matters. In Christ, you will find the meaning and purpose of your life. You will find them by meditating, praying, and reading the Bible. You will find yourself praying for others, even those who did not ask you to pray for them. You will find yourself exercising great temperance in many aspects of your life, and that temperance is increasing day after day. You will find yourself dealing kindly and gently with those who mistreat you. You will find yourself blessing those who hurt and curse you. You will find yourself driven by the love of God to all others in humanity. You will find yourself reciting the affirmations of the template as you taste the sweetness and the positive impact on your mind. You will find that meditation becomes the daily reflection on the Source of life that is God. You will find yourself forgiving people for their acts even without their apology. You will find yourself apologizing to those who offended you. You will find that you are selective in your words, and your words are full of wisdom and grace. You will find that you have a good grip on your thoughts and senses, and your mind does not entertain a thought that does not match Christ. You will find that Christ will be the main focus of your mind. You will find your mind functioning in Christ's grace. You will find that you are using the full capacity of your mind. You will find yourself reacting positively to peoples' negative actions. You will find yourself in a state of peace, joy, and optimism. Who couldn't be like this if Christ is his nature?

(5) Christ-like Character

We become what we meditate on. What we meditate on becomes our essence. When we mediate on Christ, He becomes our essence. When Christ becomes our essence, we become Christ-like persons. When the grace of God transforms us to be Christ-like persons, we then will have holy and pure thoughts. We will be driven by humility and meekness. Our character will be forgiving, full of tender mercies and kindness. We will have the peace of Christ guarding our minds. We will process our lives through Christ's wisdom. Only then, will we overcome the world as He overcame the world. When we become Christ-like persons, we manifest to the world that we are sons and daughters of God. When we act as sons and daughters of God, we will glorify our Heavenly Father, and the world will see our good deeds and glorify our Father in heaven.

Dear reader, the template of meditation presented in this entire book is available on the following one page. To put this template into practical use, it is an excellent idea to make several copies of it. Then, put those templates inside plastic cover sheets in accessible places, and start to recite the meditation on a regular basis. If you have a Christ-like spiritual routine, incorporate mediation into that practice. If you don't have one, use this template as a starting point. If your spiritual disciplines are at a higher level than this template, kindly pray for those who use it to achieve the benefits of it. When you start practicing meditation, the human Adversary may try to convince you that it does not make sense. I encourage you to persevere until you reap fruits from your continuous effort. Your life is yours to change, and God will give you grace to do so. You have one life to live. Meditation is a magnificent tool that will make your willpower strong, will increase your awareness, will restore balance into your life, and will make you accept the present while working to have a good future. Meditation on Christ's teachings is a practice by your free will with which you program your subconscious mind for God's good will. When you find this book between your hands, kindly know that it is the grace of God that brought it to you that you may have a magnificent life. God bless you!

We become what we meditate on.
When we meditate on Christ, Christ becomes our essence.

In Christ Meditation

\+ *In Christ, I Am a (son, daughter) of God. Christ lives in me and loves me. Christ is my Strength, Peace, and Salvation. Christ is greater than the world. I think what Christ would think, I say what Christ would say; I do what Christ wants me to do. Glory to God.*

1. *In Christ, I Am Purity. I feel God; I feel Good.*
2. *In Christ, I Am Love. I love God and His Creation.*
3. *In Christ, I have Strong Faith. I trust God; I have no Fear.*
4. *In Christ, I Am Humbleness and Thanksgiving. I Am Obedience.*
5. *In Christ, I Am Wisdom and Discernment. I Am Silence.*
6. *In Christ, I control my Thoughts and my Senses. I Am Focused.*
7. *In Christ, I Am Patience, Perseverance, Positivity, and Persistence. I Am Accuracy and Understanding.*

\+ *In Christ, I Am a (son, daughter) of God. Christ lives in me and loves me. Christ is my Strength, Peace, and Salvation. Christ is greater than the world. I think what Christ would think, I say what Christ would say; I do what Christ wants me to do. Glory to God.*

1. *In Christ, I Am Optimism. I have Hope and Willpower.*
2. *In Christ, I Am Calmness and Confidence. I Am Gentleness.*
3. *In Christ, I Am Compassion and Forgiveness. I Am Mercy.*
4. *In Christ, I Am Prosperity. I have Abundance. I Am Kindness.*
5. *In Christ, I Am Comfort and Healing. I Am the Solution.*
6. *In Christ, I Am Healthy and Wealthy. I have Strong Memory.*
7. *In Christ, I overcome illnesses and spirits. I overcome myself. I Am a new (man, woman). I Am Christ-like.*

\+ *In Christ, I Am a (son, daughter) of God. Christ lives in me and loves me. Christ is my Strength, Peace, and Salvation. Christ is greater than the world. I think what Christ would think, I say what Christ would say; I do what Christ wants me to do. Glory to God.*

References

1. "Saint Augustine Quotes." BrainyQuote.com. BrainyMedia Inc, 2020. 20 December 2020. https://www.brainyquote.com/quotes/saint_augustine_148546
2. Allen, James. "The Power of Meditation." *As a Man Thinketh; From Poverty to Power*. Ed. Arthur R. Pell. Penguin Group, 2008. 133-34. Print.
3. Murphy, Joseph. "The Conscious and Subconscious Minds." *The Power of Your Subconscious Mind*. Wilder Publications, 2007. 16. Print.
4. Coué, Émile. "Conscious Autosuggestion." *Self Mastery Through Conscious Autosuggestion*. Digireads.com Publishing, 2006. 15. Print.
5. "Saint Augustine Quotes." BrainyQuote.com. BrainyMedia Inc, 2020. 20 December 2020. https://www.brainyquote.com/quotes/saint_augustine_121380
6. Thomas, Kempis A. "Imitating Christ and Despising All Vanities on Earth." *The Imitation of Christ*. Bruce, 1940. 4. Print.
7. Thomas, Kempis A. " Avoiding Idle Talk." *The Imitation of Christ*. Bruce, 1940. 10. Print.
8. Pope Shenouda III. "Your Name Is Ointment Poured Forth." Have You Seen the One I Love? Contemplations on the Song of Songs. Book-Surge, 2004. 54. Print.
9. "Helen Keller Quotes." BrainyQuote.com. BrainyMedia Inc, 2020. 20 December 2020. https://www.brainyquote.com/quotes/helen_keller_120988
10. "Francis of Assisi Quotes." BrainyQuote.com. BrainyMedia Inc, 2020. 20 December 2020. https://www.brainyquote.com/quotes/francis_of_assisi_121023
11. "Unknown Quotes." BrainyQuote.com. BrainyMedia Inc, 2021. 1 June 2021. https://www.brainyquote.com/quotes/unknown_106287
12. Teresa, Mother. "On Giving." *No Greater Love / Mother Teresa*. New World Library, 1997. 44. Print.
13. "Francis of Assisi Quotes." BrainyQuote.com. BrainyMedia Inc, 2021. 4 January 2021. https://www.brainyquote.com/quotes/francis_of_assisi_121465

14."Saint Augustine Quotes." BrainyQuote.com. BrainyMedia Inc, 2021. 1 June 2021. https://www.brainyquote.com/quotes/saint_augustine_148556

15.Peale, Norman Vincent. "Positive Secrets of Health and Energy." *Why Some Positive Thinkers Get Powerful Results*. Ballantine, 1986. 158. Print.

16."Mahatma Gandhi Quotes." BrainyQuote.com. BrainyMedia Inc, 2020. 22 December 2020. https://www.brainyquote.com/quotes/mahatma_gandhi_109075

17."The Practice of the Presence of God Quotes by Brother Lawrence." Goodreads, www.goodreads.com/work/quotes/2133549-maximes-spirituelles.

About the Author

Malak Morgan earned his doctorate degree in pharmacy from the University of Florida. He published his first book Always & Never that is a synopsis of wisdom with the intent to improve the quality of life of his readers. The current manuscript, In Christ Meditation, is his recommended spiritual practice of meditating on Christ. It is based on biblical Scriptures and vivid personal life experience, as well as observations and analyses of human behavior. The intent of the practice is that a man can take God's word and ingrain it in his mind and heart, and through the grace of God and the work of the Holy Spirit become a Christ-like person. It is then a man can find true joy and fulfillment in his life. It is then he can overcome the challenges of this life as Christ did.

Malak completed writing this book during the 2020 pandemic that challenged the entire world. The importance of this aspect is that he is able to put the principles laid in this book into practice. God is always in peace. As God is taking care of the birds of the sky, He will take care of us. We, as sons and daughters of God, are expressions of God's peace on earth. God is the Whole peace and we are part of His peace. While this question was going around: why is there a pandemic? By living the meditation on Christ, the author finds the answer. God does everything with a sense of purpose. There is always a positive side to every event. It depends on which side we would look. In a humble view of the pandemic, it is a period for humanity to slow down. Our brothers and sisters in Christ who left the world are now in the presence of the Lord forever. Those who lost their jobs, God sent them help and sustained them. Scientists stood up and produced the vaccine. On a personal level, the author learned how to make masks, and provided them while there were shortages at the beginning of the pandemic.

The author deeply believes that all humans are just branches in one tree called humanity. On this basis, he provides this manuscript to tell his brothers and sisters in humanity how they can change their lives as he did. The author earned a doctorate degree, got married and is blessed with two boys. He also published a book with more to come. He has found the secret of how to carry on all these challenges after surviving a severe heart condition. The secret is to meditate on Christ. Meditation on Christ makes man receptive to the grace of God and the work of the Holy Spirit. Then God's grace transforms man into Christ-likeness. Only then, when we become Christ-like persons, can we carry on difficult tasks, find joy and fulfillment; hence, our lives become magnificent.

Made in the USA
Columbia, SC
06 November 2023

25186154R00115